# Knots Made Good:
# Sailing Adventures in Eastern Canada

# Knots Made Good:
# Sailing Adventures in Eastern Canada

## Eric North
Forward by Don Currie
Artwork and Editing by Jennifer Bass

2015

Copyright © 2016 Next View Publishing

For the purposes of this copyright notice, this book and any portion thereof, "all rights reserved" applies to all content in this book notwithstanding specific portions identified within the text of this book as having separate copyright and licensing specified under the Creative Commons Attribution-ShareAlike License. This book or any portion thereof may not be reproduced or used in any manner whatsoever without the express written permission of the publisher and copyright holder except for the use of brief quotations in a book review or scholarly journal.

Portions obtained from Wikipedia® within the text of this book are subject to the Creative Commons Attribution-ShareAlike License. License is available at: https://creativecommons.org/licenses/by-sa/3.0/.

Select sailing terminology in the glossary of this book is used with permission and is graciously made available by: http://www.schoolofsailing.net/terminology.html.

First Printing: 2015
Second Printing: 2016

ISBN 978-0-9939747-0-0

Next View Publishing
567 Elm Court
Cold Lake, Alberta   T9M 2C2
Canada

www.nextviewpublishing.com

# Dedication

To my wife Christine, for putting up with me being away at sea on numerous occasions since we first met.

# Contents

| | |
|---|---|
| Acknowledgements | ix |
| Forward by Don Currie | xi |
| Introduction | 1 |
| Ch 1: Halifax, NS to Kingston, ON | 5 |
| Ch 2: Québec, QC to Baddeck, NS | 47 |
| Ch 3: Charlottetown, PEI to Ste Anne-des-Monts, QC | 65 |
| Ch 4: Québec, QC to Rimouski, QC | 77 |
| Ch 5: Kingston, ON to McGregor Bay, ON | 87 |
| Ch 6: Gaspé, QC to Québec, QC | 113 |
| Ch 7: Pigeon Island Race, Kingston, ON | 133 |
| Epilogue | 137 |
| Appendix 1: Maritimes Trip | 141 |
| Appendix 2: McGregor Bay Trip | 145 |
| Appendix 3: Bagatelle - A Living History | 149 |
| References | 151 |
| Glossary | 153 |

# Acknowledgements

One day I woke up and decided to write a book about sailing. I don't remember the exact day but it was sometime during the off-season, when boats are high out of the icy cold water and boaters begin to get the itch for warmer weather. On a cold winter day in Ontario it didn't take long for me to run with the idea of writing about several exciting and action-packed sailing trips. Armed with an old notebook full of log entries I set about putting them into the text you see in front of you.

As you'll soon find out, a decent number of people participated in these trips and each contributed their share of log entries. The entries were seasoned with both their personalities as well as past experiences aboard boats. With few exceptions, each person was on vacation and eager to make the most of their part of the adventure; more important was the fact that everyone was united in a common vision of seeing the boat reach its next destination safe and sound. To all the crew members who sailed with Bagatelle these many years, thank you for your dedication in making each trip possible.

To Don Currie for his support for this book and most importantly: years of sailing along with countless repairs, modifications and alterations to keep his boat Bagatelle afloat.

To Don's wife Sylvia, for accommodating Don's travels that kept him away over many, many summers. In addition to taking care of all affairs while Don was away, she prepared home-baked meals and treats for the Skipper and crew at their departure from Kingston each trip. These meals and desserts were most appreciated!

I owe a big thank-you to Jennifer Bass for her creative consultation, editing, proof-reading and amazing artwork throughout this book! With great insight and thoughtfulness she provided me with several detailed charts of our trips, drawn by her own hand. These charts are are an artistic depiction of Bagatelle's many travels. The charts might come in handy for people contemplating similar trips, although you will need to purchase your own nautical charts for the area you intend to sail in. I recommend keeping both paper and electronic charts when sailing. Paper can be bulky but it sure comes in handy when all of your boat's electrical systems decide to suddenly stop working.

Select sailing terminology in the glossary of this book is used with permission and is graciously made available by the School of Sailing, http://www.schoolofsailing.net/terminology.html.

Thanks also to Mike Peters for helping with proof-reading. From his experiences aboard the sailing training vessel Tuna, a lifetime of other kinds of sailing as well as working closely with boats of one description or another, Mike provided me with insightful suggestions and improvements throughout this book.

Thanks to Chris Currie for offering his permission to use several photographs during our trips, as well as his help in tracking down and reproducing a noteworthy piece of history on Bagatelle at the Marine Museum of the Great Lakes.

Photos of Bagatelle's brush with disasater in Chapter 7 are reprinted with thanks to Chief Petty Officer Shaun Perry.

Many thanks to Ms Sandrena Raymond and the Marine Museum of the Great Lakes for permitting me to replicate a text panel containing information on Bagatelle. A photograph of this panel is located in an appendix at the end of the book and provides readers with information on Bagatelle's early years.

# Forward by Don Currie

In the Summer of 2001 Eric North was introduced to salt water sailing in Bagatelle, a 41-foot sailing yacht, one of the 1969 contenders for the defence of the Canada's Cup at the Royal Canadian Yacht Club in 1969. Together with four other crew members, he began his first exposure to long distance sailing by testing his endurance to sea sickness. Enjoying visits to various ports enroute to Kingston, Ontario, Eric became addicted to the sport of sailing, particularly long distance sailing. Over the next few years Eric became very much attached to the boat, looking forward to passages that were interesting, demanding, educational and rewarding. A more reliable crew member could not be found under any conditions of weather or sickness. On a passage between PEI and Îles-de-la-Madeleine, his seasickness was extreme, yet he performed well, even though conditions were severe. Be prepared to enjoy some of his fond memories in the following pages.

# Introduction

I want to let everyone know I had little experience with sailing prior to the trips described in this book! Previous trips included a stint in a dinghy at Royal Military College of Canada (RMCC) in Kingston, ON and one evening excursion aboard a sloop at Cold Lake, AB in the summer of 2000. Fast-forward to a cold and snowy day in the spring of 2001 where I found myself on a bus to Québec City, travelling with the Pipes & Drums and Brass & Reed bands of RMCC. We stopped for a short break when Don Currie, an alumnus of Royal Roads Military College and fellow band-member approached and asked me if I'd be interested in sailing with him during the upcoming summer. He told me he's looking for crew for a round-trip voyage from Kingston to the Maritimes aboard Bagatelle, a 41-foot C&C Redline. The plan was for crew members to embark and disembark at various points along the trip. Don informed me one of his biggest challenges was finding the right combination of experienced and new people to take aboard the boat at each stop. As luck would have it, I was in Halifax with almost a month of vacation following training. By happy coincidence, Skipper and Bagatelle would be arriving in Halifax to begin their return journey to Kingston at the same time I completed my training. It didn't take me long to make my decision!

The trip from Halifax, NS to Kingston, ON that summer turned out to be more spectacular and nerve-wracking than I could have ever imagined. We sailed with a varying number of crew on the return leg of Bagatelle's voyage to the Maritimes. Everyone brought with them a unique set of perspectives and mentalities along with different degrees of sailing experience. The stops we made at so many coastal towns and villages left me with a lasting impression of their denizens' warmth, kindness and hospitality. Arriving in Kingston and getting ready to head back to school, I resolved to mark my calendar somewhere between June and September for future trips.

Many summers of sailing would follow; each trip had its share of adventures as well as hectic and challenging moments.

The following chapters are a combination of Bagatelle's log entries interspersed with my notes during our trips. Log entries appear in sans serif font as follows:

(time of log entry): (log entry). Example: "21h03: Eric acquainted with wave action which is annoying all of us in this uncomfortable sea."

Unless otherwise specified all times in this book are in 24-hour time, denoted as "HhhMM."

The last chapter is not about a trip; rather, the Pigeon Island Race in 2013 held close to Kingston, ON. Other regattas and short stints are not included in this book. For most races, the action is fast-paced. Log entries can be sparse as the Skipper and crew are too engaged in sailing.

Tables summarizing each trip are included at the end of each chapter, with the exception of Chapter 7. The Epilogue contains a table showing all trips with totals for distance, time spent on the boat, time underway and other items of interest. In addition, there are tables in two of the appendices to provide readers with information on expected round-trip distances, number of stops, required number of crew in addition to total costs.

I hope you all find this book captivating and appealing regardless if you count yourself as a seasoned mariner, land-lubber or anywhere in-between. Two perspectives permeate throughout each chapter: for the first you have to put yourself in the shoes of a person who took up sailing "by doing," learning the most critical things on-the-spot with each trip they took. The second is about all of the impressions one has in regard to Eastern Canada when viewed from the water.

After reading each chapter and for those who've never sailed before, I encourage each of you to take a trip down to your local yacht club. Once you've arrived, poke around and ask if anyone is looking for crew. There should be at least one skipper who's inclined to take someone willing, able and new aboard. If you're at this point do what you can to prepare yourself for the challenge and adventure awaiting you!

4    Knots Made Good

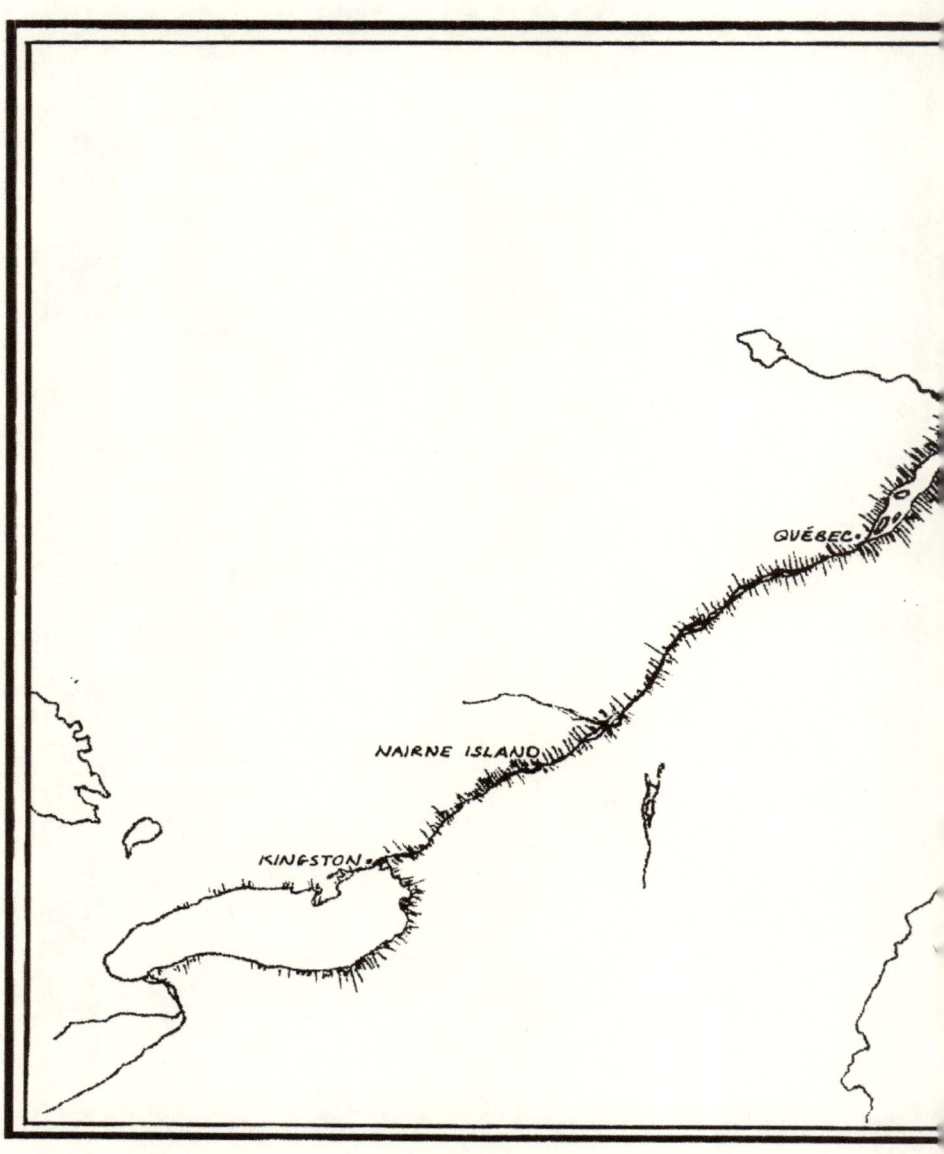

Chapter 1

*Halifax, NS to Kingston, ON*

31 July to 25 August 2001

One last-minute stop to pick up a sleeping bag in downtown Halifax is all that is between me and sailing for the remainder of the summer. Pat, a fellow crewman, offers me a ride to the Yacht Club to meet Don and the other crew. Pat is in the Royal Canadian Navy and is stationed in Halifax. He has a few days to spend aboard the boat as does another crewman named Adrian. Mark will also join us Halifax; he plans to stay aboard for the remainder of Bagatelle's journey to Kingston.

Pat and I drive to Armdale Yacht Club in an overcast afternoon. We make our way to the Yacht Club and look for Bagatelle. She is moored at one of docks farther out and not visible upon our arrival so we grab our gear and scan numerous boats while walking. I have trouble spotting Bagatelle from the grainy photo sent by Don; Pat recognizes her at first glance and we make our way on-board.

This is the return leg of Don's trip this summer. Adrian and Mark show up later while Don, Pat and I are out grocery shopping. I learn Don is somewhat particular about food aboard the boat. Garlic and yogurt are "anathema" in his opinion; however, I think I'm asked at least twice if I like liver while we're walking up and down isles. Hmm... for our first meal I offer to cook Boston bluefish and potatoes. As we finish grocery shopping I run into Darren, a classmate of mine who returned from Australia a few days ago. We talk for a few minutes then say goodbye as Don, Pat and I need to return to the boat.

Back aboard Bagatelle the four crewmen get settled in and become acquainted with her interior. Don remarks she is a bit more spartan than most boats but she is sleek, fast and built for racing! Her diesel engine resides under a teak ladder, next to the ice-box. There are two VHF hand-sets connected to a single receiver, one in the cockpit and a second below the cabin entrance. A small but sufficient double sink shares the same counter-space as the ice-box; a gimballed stove powered by propane sits forward of the sink. The gimbals are affixed along Bagatelle's longitudinal axis and thus permit sailors to operate the stove when the boat is running through rough seas or is heeled to port or starboard.

Don making a few notes in Bagatelle's log before we depart Armdale Yacht Club.

Sliding Plexiglas for the lockers above the sink and latch-able doors are affixed to other lockers to keep goods in place during rough seas. Plenty of storage space for provisions, ship's gear, clothing and personal items. There are several sleeping quarters, the first is the quarter berth and according to Don is the most comfortable as it is farthest aft. While experience will prove him correct in terms of minimum wave action, I can't help but disagree on account of the engine and transmission located adjacent to this berth. Forward of the chart table and along each side amidships are two generous berths, one of which is over top one of Bagatelle's diesel fuel tanks. Moving farther forward, we find the head on her port side and a set of generous lockers on her starboard side. Still farther forward and there is a large plexiglas hatch above two berths with a decent amount of storage space below them. There are several round lamps in the head as well as in proximity to each berth, each with their own toggle switches and powered from the deep-cycle house batteries kept in water-tight containers and located under one of the lockers in the cockpit.

Before casting off, Don acquaints me with Bagatelle's electrical systems including a small belt-driven pump that comes on when someone opens the sink tap. A whaling pump sits next to the sink taps and I find out later it is used a lot more than the electric pump to conserve batteries. The bilge is accessible by a removable teak panel in-laid in the floorboards between the two berths amidships. Other crew and I get briefed on keeping periodic watch on the bilge along with some quick instructions on how to purge it. The other items Don walks us through are circuit breakers above the ice-box along with a number of switches and a battery indicator with push-to-test button to check the charge of each set of house batteries.

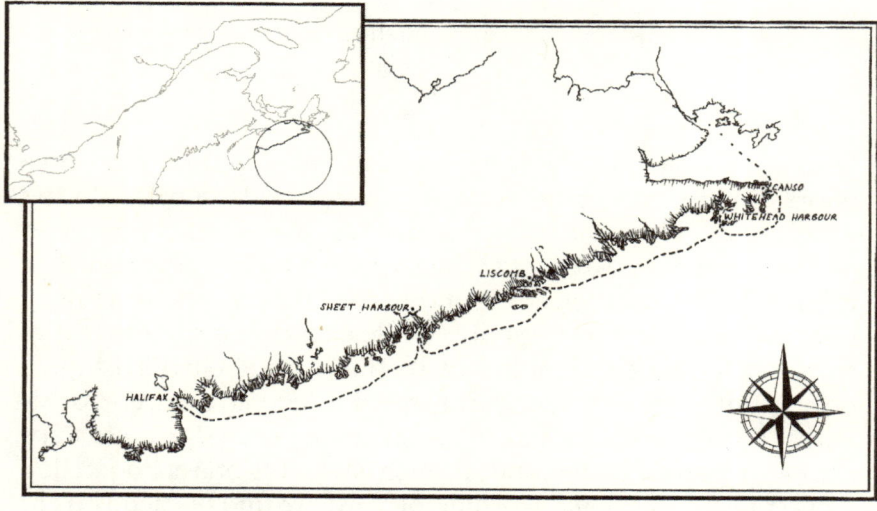

The first portion of Bagatelle's return to Kingston, ON. Our east-bound course is from Halifax to Sheet Harbour, then to Liscombe, then Whitehead Harbour followed by Canso, NS.

## 31 July 2001, Halifax to Sheet Harbour

We slip Armdale at 18h40 and after getting a good view of Halifax from the harbour I head below to get to work on supper. The propane stove comes to life with the help of a barbecue lighter and pretty soon the fish and potatoes are underway. Seas are almost a flat calm as we leave the harbour but once past McNabs Island the wind and waves pick up. Cheerful at the prospect of spending the best part of my summer aboard this fine boat I'm oblivious to the smells of inexpensive fish, propane and a number of as-of-yet-indescribable aromas. In her decades of service, Bagatelle sees thousands of nautical miles (NM) of ocean and Great Lakes with scores of crew toiling aboard. Various fluids reside in her bilge from engine and transmission, infusing the cabin with a sharp scent. Coupled with multiple sources of odour such as kerosene lamps, a propane stove, lockers full of diesel-soaked clothing and numerous un-washed personal articles the result is a collective scent clinging to anyone and anything spending more than five minutes aboard.

After forty-five minutes of serving the crew their dinner I sense a slight queasiness: Pat offers to finish cooking the meal. Heading topside I have a few minutes to catch the last of a glorious sunset. Halifax is well behind us and we're out in the open ocean. Although the waves have increased my appetite usurps any feeling of discomfort from the seas. After finishing the last few bites of my supper my stomach is in a bad place! Heading port-side I reach over the top lifeline and commit my meal to the sea, down-wind. Lifelines are the set of braided cables that run along Bagatelle's port and starboard edges, held up by stanchions. Crew secure their personal harnesses to these cables in rough seas, clipping and re-clipping as they make their way forward or aft. Both harnesses and lifelines are worth their weight in gold many times over on our trips.

Feeling much better I sip water from one of Don's faded yellow melamine cups and think the worst is behind me. Wrong! For the rest of the night and well into the next day I'm over Bagatelle's sides once every fifteen minutes with the precision of a Swiss watch. As the sky darkens we move farther and farther into the choppy sea, I'm getting more and more experience with sea-sickness.

21h03: Eric acquainted with wave action which is annoying all of us in this uncomfortable sea.

My muscles sing with aches and pains as I bring up less and less of the contents of my stomach each time, tears streaming down my cheeks. Not from crying for the sake of crying but from the tension in my face as it contorts into various grotesque shapes. This awfulness doesn't abate and I get precious few minutes after each bout as I crouch at Bagatelle's cabin door. Water refuses to stay down; I get little relief and the breeze while cold is my comfort. I'm an impediment to the other crew as they make their way in and out of the cabin: they're patient and I do my best to make way. Perched along the edges of the cockpit and forward of the helm, Don's twin compasses glow through the inky blackness, small reassurances we're all alive out in this vast expanse of ocean but at the same time forcing us to realize we are alone in our journey. Mark is at the helm and fighting to make the best of 6 to 10 knots (kt) of wind with a reef. Reefing points run parallel to the bottom of Bagatelle's main sail and permit us to lower a portion and secure it to the boom using reefing lines. One or more reefing points are useful in stronger winds when we want to reduce the cross-section of the main as opposed to changing it out for a smaller one. Putting in a reef aboard Bagatelle can be challenging in rough weather and we therefore make them in advance of storms or heavy wind despite some loss of speed should weather not take a turn for the worse.

Heading down below I notice Adrian has taken a few Gravol and is out cold, much to Pat's chagrin and frustration since he's forced to do a double-shift. I'm sick as soon as my feet touch the cabin floor and I scurry for the head (bathroom) hoping to arrive before my mouth explodes. I'm through the door to the head when it happens. Coming forward to observe the goings-on, Pat informs me he "doesn't want to be an Asshole but you'll have to clean up all your mucous and stomach fluid once you're finished." It's all

I can do to quell the turmoil in my gut as I finish cleaning. Hurling myself aft I make my way topside and then heave again. And again. And... Again. Intolerable!

22h02: lumpy sea and little wind and even less progress, so operating engine at 2100 RPM.

23h45: crazy tacking almost 180°,.... But the boat is singing, it's happy. Bagatelle's mast emits a pleasant "hum" when her sails are trimmed, she's heeled over and making good progress on a tack.

## 01 August 2001, Enroute to Sheet Harbour

00h50: winds are up around 15-20 kt, Mark is turning over with Adrian, Eric is still taking fresh air, Don is sleeping.

04h38: tug passed by (close) on starboard towing something. It overtook us at close range. Most disconcerting as we had our hands full with the strong wind.

I move in and out of consciousness as dawn begins to replace the darkness. I'm aware of the sun casting it's rays across the boat as we head for calmer waters and make for Sheet Harbour. I'm frozen in place and muttering to myself as we secure at the wharf.

13h08: secure at Sheet Harbour wharf at north-east arm at public wharf, walked into town about a mile or so.

After making fast to the wharf I make my way below and have a glorious sleep. I awake later in the day and we all agree to head to a small store up the road. Don decides to keep Bagatelle and crew at the harbour for the remainder of the day and slip the following morning. He tells me later this whole business of me being sick is worrisome as for sure he thought I'd be begging to head back to Halifax on land and never want to set sail again!

## 02 August 2001, Sheet Harbour to Liscombe Harbour

10h11: slipped wharf in Sheet Harbour's north-east arm.

11h50: decide to fly a spinnaker, but discover the spinnaker pole has disappeared. It must have gone overboard during the heavy weather on Tuesday night. Don is pissed off!

Pat takes me aside during the afternoon to talk about marine navigation. I get acquainted with several instruments aboard Don's boat including the radar, LORAN,[1] GPS, ship's log and several compasses. Don's main compass, forward of the chart table, is a generous 12" in diameter and is enclosed in a large clear dome. Pat instructs me in taking readings from the LORAN and then plotting a fix on our present chart. We're on a steady course thanks to a decent wind aft of the boat: I'm directed to plot our course using our present fix plus heading. It takes me a few attempts to use the parallels and the compass rose on the chart but Pat is confident I have the hang of it after a few attempts. A good navigator is diligent in plotting fixes at regular intervals, both on the chart and in the boat's log. Unless the boat is close to shore and sailing in familiar water we need to know where we are and where we're headed in the event of a power failure. Pat enforces in me the need to be "proactive" when sailing.

19h19: secure at Liscombe Lodge dock and fuelled. Two other boats came to mooring later.

Liscombe Lodge is a good stop, our first opportunity for showers since Halifax. The pool and two hot tubs are nice: we have to cut our time short after a wrestling match leaves Mark's nose bloody and Pat's eye swollen. The paddle-boats are a welcome diversion to finish off the evening and then we head for our berths to make the best of a fresh start the following day. Before we sleep, Pat

---

[1] LORAN, or LOng RAnge Navigation is a hyperbolic radio navigation system developed in the United States during World War II. It was first used for ship convoys crossing the Atlantic Ocean and later by long-range patrol aircraft. The definition in this foot-note is licensed under a Creative Commons Attribution 3.0 License, original work copyright Wikipedia®: LORAN, http://en.wikipedia.org/wiki/LORAN, January 2015.

takes me through another crash-course on navigation using the charting program on Don's computer, setting way-points and route for our departure and reminding me about being proactive.

## 03 August 2001, Liscombe to Canso

08h52: slipped Liscombe Lodge.

I'm still in my berth when Bagatelle gets underway, the sun is shining as we get ready to hit the open water and make sail. Adrian tells me I've missed an awesome breakfast at Liscombe Lodge: I remain content in having had a few extra minutes of sleep. We're soon out at sea and under sail with a gentle wind. The sun casts its warmth throughout the day and the boat is making

A clear and sunny afternoon, perfect sailing weather!

good progress as we head eastward. I'm out in the cockpit enjoying a pleasant afternoon at sea, waves rolling with a steady breeze and clear skies. Bagatelle's wind-powered battery charger (herein referred to as the "wind charger") sparks to life with the steady gusts on our stern. It emits a loud "hiss" and sways from side-to-side with each change in wind direction. With all of these sights and sounds ingrained in my memory I consider the classes I'll be in later this fall, knowing I'll be sitting at a desk thinking back to this day.

17h45: arrive at Whitehead Harbour.

Don decides to make for shelter at Whitehead since adverse weather is approaching from the south-west. He takes back the helm and directs the crew to prepare for entry into the harbour. I seat myself at the chart table, keeping a watchful eye on our course as we head for the inlet. Bringing my gaze up to the green glow of the radar's screen my heart skips a beat as this massive, malevolent blob of storm quickly moves in on our stern. I have enough time to grab Bagatelle's cabin doors from the locker beside the ladder, secure both doors with a rag-tag assortment of pins and then swing them shut before the wall of rain reaches us. And what a wall! Pelting the boat with an incredible fury the torrential downpour makes its way through tiny slats in each door and soaks all food stored below the ladder. Myself and the now wet crew make land with less than 500 yards' visibility with all eyes on nasty-looking rocks dead-ahead. The boat is jostled by big waves as we make our way to the shelter and sanctity of the harbour. Don calls out for the crew to spot forward and help direct him to the dock: I'm struck at his ability to handle Bagatelle in this rough weather! We make our way to our mooring without incident. Once secured, Mark makes good on an earlier promise to catch fish. Searching through a number of containers for some fishing line and hooks, he goes top-side. A few minutes later he manages to snag a mackerel! We ponder over whether or not to keep it as bait then throw it back overboard when we realize there's no place to store it on the boat.

After supper, someone pulls out a deck of cards and we all agree to play "Asshole." Don keeps getting confused about the order of each hand; we resolve all mistakes need to be re-mediated through drinking. Pat keeps uncorking the rum while Mark goads "what beats three sevens Don?"

Mark says goodbye to his new "friend" before throwing it overboard.

## 04 August 2001, Whitehead Harbour to Canso

07h30: slipped, no wind so motoring all the way to Canso.

This is a new sea for me; no wind whatsoever and a flat calm are out-of-place from our trip over the past few days. I'm struck by how quiet it is out in the open ocean apart from the rhythmic thud of Bagatelle's engine and prop shaft. The water is glass and we can see quite far in all directions under a bright and sunny morning. I'm aware of the boat's long and drawn-out rocking motion as we make our way through the gentleness, and can't help but become a bit lethargic.

Pat moving into position to get a couple of photos on a buoy.

09h45: I got my picture on the can, Buoy P20. My trip is now complete. Thanks Don.

With an almost flat calm and clear skies, Pat resolves to get his picture taken on a buoy. Of course, we're all up for helping him get his wish. Coming up alongside I'm struck with how difficult it's going to be to get Pat on the buoy and back aboard! Despite tranquil seas we are pitching up, down a surprising amount as we make our way closer and closer, taking care not to make contact. Pat makes the jump, clambers up the side of the can and we're all thinking for a split second he's going to topple over and end up needing to be rescued. After a bit of effort he is on top of the buoy. I'm trying my best to take pictures with no sign of land in the background as Pat calls out to us but we're circling fast. Coming around we begin to edge closer while Pat moves into position. Leaping like a crazed superhero he grabs one of the shrouds and is back aboard the boat. It's the day and age of 35mm so we'll all have to wait for the trip to finish before I can get pictures developed. I promise to get Pat copies as soon as they're ready.

12h07: secure downtown Canso (Adrian leaves for Moncton).

Coming into Canso at lunch in a calm sea, we secure at the public wharf and make for town. Adrian has to return home and gives his regards to all of us as he departs. With Bagatelle secured we head for one of the few remaining fisheries in the harbour: as luck has it at least one boat arrives with a fresh catch of snow crab. We put in a request and are provided with a generous portion, the crabs are still moving as the fisherman prepares them and then hands Mark and I several pounds of gigantic snow crab legs. We're both happy with the price he charges. Heading back to Bagatelle we make plans for supper; Don has a big enough pot so we can cook our prized meal safely. We get back just in time to

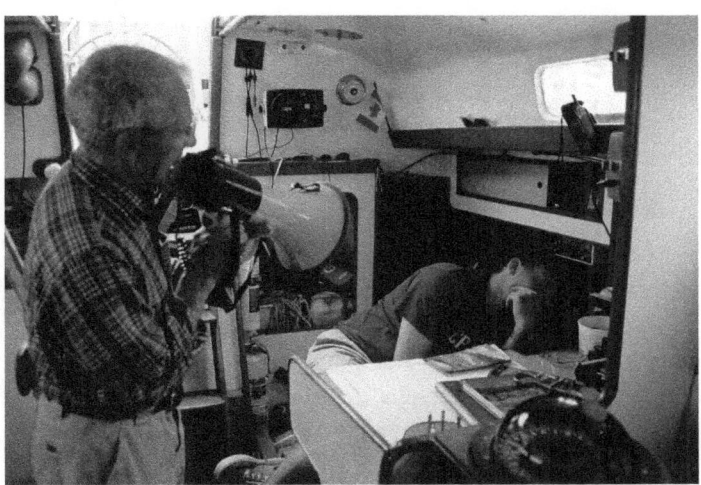

Everyone gets at least one wake-up call from the loud-hailer on our trip!

take a quick picture of Don giving Pat a "wake-up call" with the loud-hail-er. This handy piece of kit comes equipped with a siren. Pat rockets out of his slumber in no time!

Heading into town for groceries we make a quick stop at the museum. We learn there are several Viking settlements across the harbour on a small parcel of land. The girl at the counter is accommodating in telling us about her town and I admit later I'm a bit smitten. Mark wastes no time rubbing it in and I get to hear a high-pitched rendition of myself over-and-over saying "awwwwwwww she's the nicest girl I ever met awwwwww" for the rest of the bloody day.

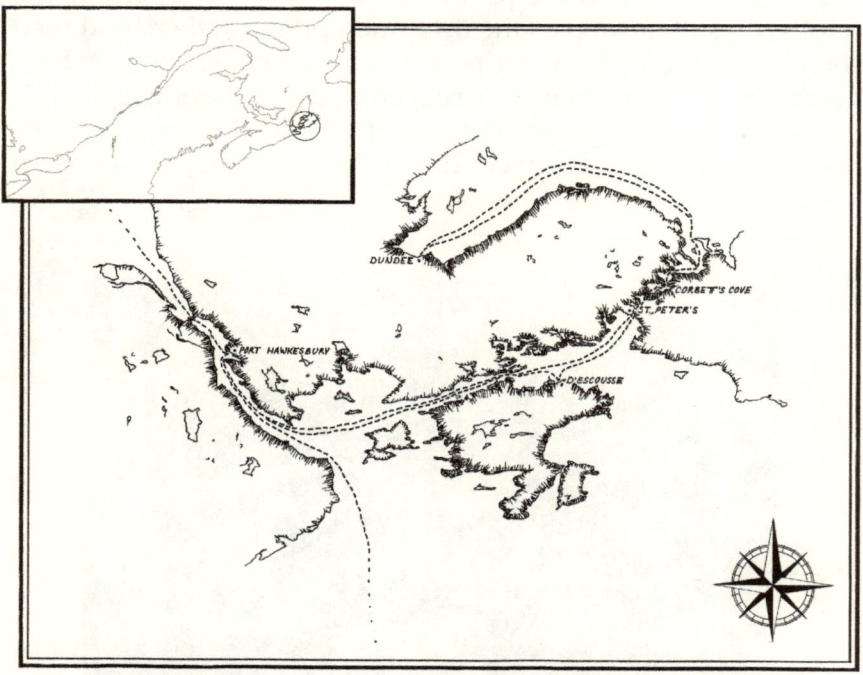

The second portion of Bagatelle's return to Kingston, ON. We proceed northward to Port Hawkesbury, east to St Peter's via D'Escousse, into the Bras d'Or Lake to Dundee then back to Port Hawkesbury, NS.

## 05 August 2001, Canso to D'Escousse

06h50: Don, Eric, Mark and Pat slipped in fog, under power, no wind.

11h30: arrive at Port Hawkesbury. Pat leaves to walk 6 miles for a bus, the alternative is to pay someone $80.00 to get back to Halifax from Canso.

Each crew-member must make their own arrangements for transport to/from Bagatelle. Most are constrained by time and often depart sooner than they'd prefer since the boat often heads farther away from their intended destination or when the arrival at the boat's next stop is uncertain.

13h00: Don, Eric and Mark slipped, wind picks up. Eric's first experience with tacking while not being debilitated by sea-sickness; we had the wind behind us for the first part of our trip. It takes much longer to get anywhere when you travel in huge zig-zags.

19h00: arrive and anchored in 18 ft of water. We can see a beach party on shore and figure it's worth checking out after supper.

We finish supper and then get Baguette ready to make for shore. "Baguette" is the name of the dinghy kept aboard Bagatelle and serves as one of her lifeboats. In places where Bagatelle is at anchor, Baguette doubles as a skiff for transporting crew to and from shore. Lighting on the shore we walk up to the Yacht Club, grab quick showers and then head to what we later learn is D'Escousse's annual gathering. People bring various instruments and everyone joins in singing and dancing. I grab a guitar and end up breaking three strings before the evening is over. Dawn is upon us when we head back in Baguette close to 04h30 with a number of items Mark picks up from the party including strings of Christmas lights, citronella candles, several pairs of sunglasses, cigarettes, an ice bucket and numerous miscellany. He's telling me not to worry in-between wearing three pairs of shades and singing at the top of his lungs as we make our way aboard Bagatelle.

## 06 August 2001, D'Escousse to St Peter's

13h00: slipped.

14h30: arrive at St Peter's Canal and tie up.

The lock operator informs us we have a few hours before we can proceed to the other side and into the Bras d'Or Lakes. After the large rain squall outside of Whitehead Harbour none of us have had a chance to dry some of the clothing and berth mattresses that got wet. After arranging all of these articles on-deck before we head into town, Mark remarks that we look like an "immigrant ship." Making our way up from the locks, the town of St Peter's is picturesque and inviting. We tour a museum, stop to buy groceries then head back to the locks for them to open at 19h00. Passing through, we make for one of the coves to anchor for the night. We arrive at Corbett's cove near Beaver Island at 19h40 and drop anchor in 21 ft of water. Calm and peaceful out here!

## 07 August 2001, Corbett's Cove to Dundee

08h30: slipped.

The sun is shining through broken cloud as we head into the Bras d'Or Lake. I'm happy to be at the wheel and learning more about Bagatelle's systems, including the autohelm. It contains an electronic compass as a reference for setting a course. There is a control and display unit located beside Bagatelle's wheel, on the port side. Crew can enter their desired course using either a rotary dial or push-buttons. Underneath the deck of the cockpit, an electrically-driven hydraulic pump powers a ram. The ram pushes and pulls mechanical linkages connected to the boat's rudder. In calm seas and with the autohelm engaged, the ram makes small corrections to keep Bagatelle on course. When conditions worsen and seas get rougher, the autohelm will cycle the rudder from one stop to the other. This action requires a lot of power and Don instructs us to use the autohelm with the engine on when we're in rough water. Too much usage without the engine will kill the batteries.

On a steady course to Marble Mountain, Don elects to bring us to Dundee Marina for fuel as it is one of few spots in this area where he can replenish. We alter course and make our way to the marina under sail.

13h30: arrive at Dundee Marina; 2 litres (L) of gasoline is introduced into the reserve tank which is about 3/4 full.

The gasoline incident is something else! A few minutes passes before Don asks the attendant what type of fuel he's putting into the forward tank. It isn't obvious by the colour of the nozzle and we're all mortified to learn Bagatelle is getting topped up with gas instead of diesel. I borrow Don's cell phone and call my stepfather to ask if everything will be okay. At the time of our trip he operates an excavating business with the majority of his equipment being diesel-powered: "No way! You could get away with a bit of diesel going into a gas engine, it wouldn't run great but it would run. Gas in a diesel engine on the other hand will ruin

Mark and Don double-check which fuel nozzle is used after several hours of purging Bagatelle's forward tank.

it." So we're left with no choice but to purge the tank. This is challenging since the forward tank isn't in a convenient spot and there's not much access within the bowels of the boat. The inlet is located topside so we have to resort to near partial dismantlement to remove the offending fuel. De-fuelling is slow-going and after several hours we get all of the contents purged including the length of line running topside. Once refuelled we prepare to depart, although now we have to head back to St Peter's as opposed to making for Marble Mountain on the Bras d'Or Lake. Too much time spent at Dundee Marina for any more sailing and exploring in this part of Cape Breton Island. We'll explore this part of Cape Breton another time perhaps.

16h30: slipped from Dundee Marina and put in a reef with the working jib.

Leaving the sanctity of Dundee Marina we're soon under sail and making for the south inlet of the lake, a steady wind helping us. Mark is checking the depth and calling out "oh yeah, the depth is fine, stay to starboard of that buoy." Don's charting program quits without warning and a split second later we run aground! Fantastic. We manage to budge Bagatelle out into open water and I resume troubleshooting the charting program. A loose wire in the connector to the GPS is to blame; I ask if there's any chance of there being a soldering iron on-board. Of course, there is one. This is my first realization we're well kitted out on this trip, including food and ship's provisions tucked away in so many nooks and crannies, anchors galore, reams of charts, ropes and hundreds if not thousands of cubic feet of sail. In addition, Don has a ready supply of tools, repair parts and many odds-and-ends "just in case." In the coming years I learn from Chris (Don's son) about a few items that need to be on-board at all times: PTBKP or "paper towel, bread, ketchup and potatoes." With all tools and repair parts spread across the chart table I get to work re-soldering the offending wire and soon the charting program is up-and-running. Meanwhile Mark prepares supper: roast duck and yams picked up in St Peter's are tasty. Mark doesn't cook much but he out-does himself this meal.

20h40: arrive at St Peter's Canal Dock; mosquitoes are terrible! Had an offer to get a drive up for groceries.

## 08 August 2001, St Peter's to Port Hawkesbury via Lennox Passage

08h30: left lock under sail.

10h02: sails down, arrive at Burnt Island Bridge.

The wind and current make Don nervous as we approach Burnt Island Bridge; it seems to take forever to open.

It is a clear and sunny morning as we approach Burnt Island Bridge. The wind picks up and we're having difficulty controlling the boat's position in this current. Don has us down sails as a precaution, swinging us into the wind. The sails luff back and forth as we wrestle to get them down. Under power and expecting the bridge will open any second, we move closer and closer. Still no movement and Don is starting to get annoyed! I jump forward, heading for the pulpit with the loud-hail-er. Radio communication doesn't seem to work and we're on the verge of running aground when I'm able to shout loud enough for the operator to go to channel 16 on VHF. We learn he's waiting for a second boat to arrive before raising the bridge; this other boat is at least 3 NM away when we first arrive and crew are getting frustrated. After an intolerable pause the rusty arm swings skyward and then we head for Port Hawkesbury.

15h30: secure at Port Hawkesbury.

We don't have a lot of time for shopping as most of the stores will close soon. Mark and I are positive we encounter one of the people we partied with at D'Escousse: he doesn't talk to us, maybe because he's mad Mark made off with a bunch of tent booty on our way out. Getting back to the marina, Don, Mark and I decide to hit the bars after supper. We come across The Covered Wagon, a karaoke place full of people. Several girls start dancing when we sing so I'm thinking my voice is amazing, or more likely, everyone is drunk.

## 09 August 2001, Port Hawkesbury to Charlottetown

08h00: slipped, little to no wind.

13h30: frustrating because wind on the nose and tidal effects make for slow going! We pass Cape George and head for south-central Prince Edward Island (PEI).

I get my head down for an afternoon nap, the wind shifts during the afternoon and we're making good progress when I awake. Sun is fast sinking into the horizon and bringing an end to another glorious day of sailing. The Northumberland Strait is a nice passage and we are making good time towards Charlottetown. Moving into night-fall we cast our gaze skyward in awe at an incredible meteor shower!

## 10 August 2001, At Charlottetown

03h08: secure Charlottetown Yacht Club with welcome aid of night watchman flashing a light on their elaborate floating dock.

New crew arrive today to augment Bagatelle for the last portion of her journey: Dan shows up in the morning, Mike makes his way to the boat a bit later. After shopping we now have $130.00 worth of groceries and $130.00 worth of booze to tide us over for the next few days. Don and I head into town after supper; the mall is decent and we stop by Confederation building on our way back to the boat. Crew, minus Don, head for the bars: there's a well-painted blue line running from the yacht club to the door of one of them to make it as easy as possible on the return trip. Mike buys us rounds, pretty generous since he's on the heel of a speeding ticket and plane ticket en route to Charlottetown. Despite the drinks I'm not happy when he points out my white sports socks and sandals to everyone.

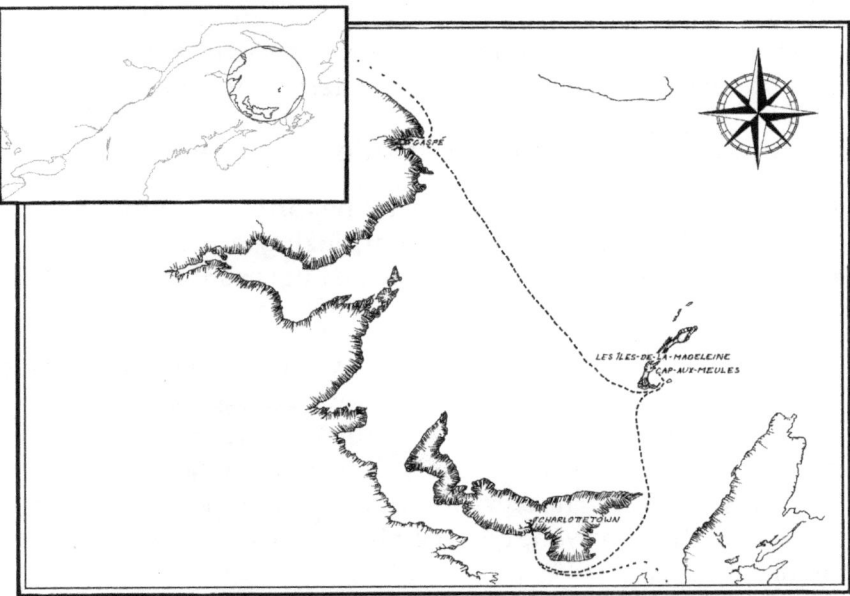

The third portion of Bagatelle's return to Kingston, ON. We depart Port Hawkesbury, NS (not shown) and head north-west towards Charlottetown, PEI, followed by Îles-de-la-Madeleine and then Gaspé, QC.

## 11 August 2001, Charlottetown to Îles-de-la-Madeleine

03h15: Don, Eric, Mark, Dan and Mike slipped.

Mark convinces Don we need to get underway right after coming back from the bar. For whatever reason Don goes along with it so we're out in the inky black night casting off and making for open water. I resolve to get my head down once everything is secure and we're underway.

09h20: the apparent wind is up to 22 kt, speed-over-ground (SoG) is over 8 kt so a single reef is put in.

15h45: second reef in main and storm jib raised.

19h39: decide to go back to working jib.

22h15: flash up engine, a clear starry night.

22h28: LORAN signal-to-noise ratio preventing its normal operation. This trouble began when the engine is started by Mark.

## 12 August 2001, Enroute to Îles-de-la-Madeleine

03h45: a strange mirage appears in the form of a plane chasing Mark at high-speed with searchlight blazing. Mark alters course and is followed by this marauder so he alters course by 180°. He finds out it is a fisherman.

In the dark of night the ocean can play tricks on people. This is brought on by the drowsiness of crew who are getting on in their midnight shift, the infinite blackness of an overcast sky and more than a few curious fishing vessels. We arrive in the wee hours at Cap-aux-Meules. The crew on-watch make Bagatelle fast to the docks and then everyone gets their head down as dawn begins to break.

06h50: secure at Cap-aux-Meules in Îles-de-la-Madeleine.

## 12 August 2001, at Cap-aux-Meules

I awake to 40's chamber music from CBC and the smell of bacon and eggs. A gorgeous morning as I make my way topside to see we're moored close to many other boats in a protected harbour. We're surrounded by hills and a gentle warming breeze brings the smell of the ocean into Bagatelle's cabin. The near-tropical weather and being in the inner sanctity of this magnificent chain of islands is something right out of a Humphrey Bogart film.

Cap-aux-Meules is a bustling town considering it is Sunday and we are on an island out in the middle of nowhere. Mark figures they trade raw goods for coconuts and virgin daughters. We come across a Tim Hortons, Radio Shack, several restaurants, grocery stores and a gigantic Sobeys distribution centre. All the women we talk to ask how long we are staying. I have a hard time saying "just one day."

## 12 August 2001, Cap-aux-Meules to Gaspé

17h30: slipped Cap-aux-Meules, have good supper.

## 13 August 2001, Enroute to Gaspé

12h00: pass through a school of dolphins with seagulls dive-bombing them. Eric not successful in filming them.

Don brings out his sextant in early afternoon and offers the crew a crash course in celestial navigation. It takes several attempts for Mark and I to each make a proper estimate of our latitude using the sun for reference.

Prior to supper and with Don below for a rest, the crew decide to lower Mark over the back of the boat for a swim while under sail. The boat is clipping along at a good pace and Mark manages to hold onto a few lines as he bangs about in the water. His swim doesn't last long as the water is cool.

17h30: house batteries are so low they are not able to start engine.

One last check to make sure we tied the safety line to the boat and then...

Mark goes for a quick swim behind Bagatelle while we're under sail.

Don's extended sleep is well-deserved as he's put in more than his fair share of night sailing in the past few days. On account of our lack of experience with Bagatelle's electrical systems, we do not realize how quick her batteries are drained by the many instruments and other equipment on-board. The wind charger keeps Bagatelle's batteries charged provided it is active. Neglecting to have it charge the batteries for the past few hours we're in a bit of trouble when I remember to visit to panel to check them. Set A is dead, set B is just as close. We manage to start the engine using the secondary batteries and then resolve to run the engine for a while until the others are charged back up. Crisis averted, dinner is served and crew joke about the state of beard growing. Mark gets rice stuck in his beard and refers to it as an "armpit on my chin."

22h23: take down the sails, no wind.

## 14 August 2001, At Gaspé

02h14: we drop anchor at Gaspé in 32 ft of water, call Québec Traffic at Rivière-au-Renard to advise completion of our sail plan.

Arriving late at night and under clear skies, Gaspé appears as a jewel-encrusted treasure with sparkling lights as we enter the inner bay. We dock as soon as practical, then get our heads down for the remainder of the night. The morning is sunny and warm; we make for town and pick up a few groceries. Mark buys the biggest piece of roast any of us have ever seen; we're not sure if it'll fit in Bagatelle's fridge never-mind her stove! Dinner ashore at "Adam's" is decent although they don't seem to get the concept of "hamburger BBQ." It arrives with a bottom half of a kaiser bun, shredded meat and sauce on top. After some tense negotiation Mark manages to convince the kitchen staff to bring him the second half of his bun. So they bring him... another bottom half. Back at the boat, two girls make their way down to the marina and ask to come aboard. These are the first women we've entertained on the boat since the start of the trip, they insist on going out with us for the evening. To top it off, our new friends keep insisting on buying us beer. It's enough to want to call Gaspé home!

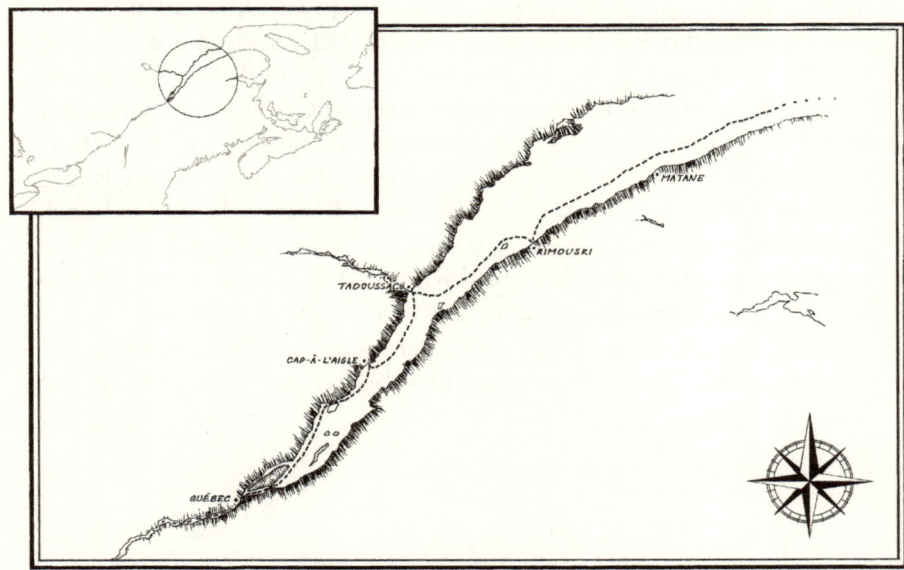

The fourth portion of Bagatelle's return to Kingston, ON. We depart Gaspé (not shown) and come around the Gaspé peninsula. Replenishing at Rimouski we proceed to Tadoussac then to Cap-à-l'Aigle and then to Québec, QC.

## 15 August 2001, Gaspé to Matane

09h30: slipped, sunny and cool, wind south-east 10 kt.

18h34: experiencing difficulties with head. It is plugged but patience managed to correct problem. A lot of patience is required.

The head (toilet) aboard Bagatelle is an interesting contraption. On a port tack, the fresh-water intake is above the water-line and will result in loss of suction when an unfortunate person "flushes." The unfortunate person has to disassemble the plumbing right where fresh water and sewage are pumped. They then have to raise the inlet hose and pour water into it to re-prime the system using a small rusty can stored in a locker under the sink. The inlet

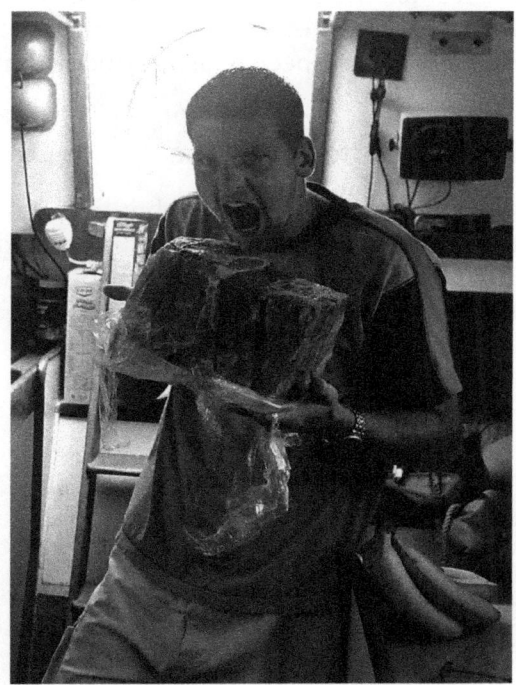

Everyone will eat a lot of meat on this trip and enjoy it. Everyone!

hose is made from heavy PVC, and thus is quite stubborn to maneuver. Moving it back down and behind to its connection point without losing any water the person then has to re-secure the hose with a finicky clamp. One may then re-attempt to purge the head. This evolution can take several attempts before successful flushing occurs. Along with a stubborn intake, the outflow valve often reverses on account of excess waste becoming clogged during discharge. One then has the penultimate pleasure of being speckled with flecks of excrement, used toilet paper and other nastiness. Since the head is located in the boat's forward section any uncomfortable motion from wave action is magnified. One's "situation" is made worse with the inevitable douse of seawater from a leaky seal around the mast. Add to all of this a rather repugnant smell in addition to being heeled over on a tack and the result is crew who elect to do their business either off the rear or front of the boat, irrespective of any and all unpleasantries due to weather!

## 16 August 2001, Enroute to Matane

Weather is decent, although cool throughout the day as we make our way north-east. Much to my consternation, large quantities of soup have to be discarded after the mixture of beans welds itself to the bottom of two of Don's pots. Despite a good soak in seawater, the beans hold fast and it takes at least two or three days before the pots are clean again.

Outside the inlet to Gaspé in the Gulf of St Lawrence, gigantic cliff faces are a sight to behold.

Heading around the Gaspé Peninsula, everyone enjoys the spectacular view along the coastline. It is remarkable to think that our earliest of explorers would have encountered these ragged cliff faces with their towering hilltops. There is a stark contrast between the lush green of trees and grey-white of the rocks. As we proceed north-west the weather gets cooler, to the point where everyone is in wet-weather gear layered with sweaters, pants and shoes. Night-time is very brisk and so the watch crew take turns at the chart table and cockpit in an effort to keep warm. These cool temperatures persist as we begin to round the Gaspé peninsula.

The wind picks up as we head towards Matane; I'm at the wheel and quite impressed with the speed we're making. Time passes before Dan comes up with a puzzled look on his face, and directs me to alter to starboard. In my ignorance I blurt out "but we're making such good time on this tack, 10 kt or more!" Both Mark and Mike have picked up on my error at this point and cry out in unison: "yeah, but in the wrong direction!" The shifting winds are altering us to port, pointing us back east!

Mike at the helm, sailing along the north-east coast of the Gaspé peninsula.

## 17 August 2001, Enroute to Rimouski

07h10: arrive at Matane. No suitable docks and too far from any conveniences. Decide to continue to Rimouski.

15h33: arrive at Rimouski.

We walk 5 miles to get to the grocery store; this isn't the nicest piece of shore as the sewage outlets are below the sidewalk. The weather is cool and rainy so we don't spend a lot of time enjoying any local attractions.

19h30: leave Rimouski.

Don at the helm with autopilot engaged, heading east on the St Lawrence.

Mike sets to work preparing an amazing meal using the gigantic roast purchased in Gaspé. Aromas from the oven and stove-top work the crew into a feeding frenzy. Sitting down to eat, we all stuff ourselves on roast beef cooked to perfection along with mashed potatoes, green beans and an awesome gravy. Thanks Mike!

## 18 August 2001, Rimouski to Tadoussac

09h30: secure at Tadoussac.

We don't have a lot of time to explore Tadoussac as the tides are in control of timings for both our arrival and departure. The fog rolls in as we make our way into town. Everyone is hoping to get a good glimpse of surroundings, but it won't happen on this trip. Other than an ancient but well cared for church we don't have much time to see anything else. Cognizant of the ebb and flow of the tide, we make our way back to the docks to depart and get a head start on several other boats. Tadoussac is situated where the Saguenay empties into the St Lawrence and the cool currents attract lots of whales. Several whale-watching tours are already heading out as we make our way back to Bagatelle.

10h08: leave Tadoussac.

20h20: arrive at Cap-à-l'Aigle.

Thanks to the tide we are stuck for a few hours, and the harbour manager at Cap-à-l'Aigle wants to charge for our stay! We manage to buy enough food to appease him and then we get ready to set sail.

22h20: leave Cap-à-l'Aigle.

## 19 August 2001, Cap-à-l'Aigle to Québec

Mark and I are on shift after leaving Cap-à-l'Aigle. I'm down at the chart table and keeping an eye on down-bound traffic while Mark is at the wheel. The night is dark as we press onwards towards Québec. Bagatelle's engine lulls me towards a state of lethargy but my senses perk up when a small, innocuous contact appears dead-ahead at 03h00. I call up to Mark to ask him if he can see a ship, he alters to port and I ask him to keep checking to see which lights are showing. With the changes in course provided, I'm expecting he's going to call "green," keeping the down-bound ship to starboard. This part of the channel is quite narrow; neither vessel has much quarter to yield. Although Mark is moving us to port, the oncoming ship is not going to pass us as expected. We alter farther to port; the south edge of the channel is getting closer with each turn of the boat's propeller. Mark calls out he can see a red light on the tanker's bow, putting us on a collision course. As it turns out, while we've altered to port the down-bound vessel is altering starboard!

Before we have time to do anything else the gigantic ship is looming up through the darkness: we're aware she's dry (empty), her decks tower above us. I'm standing at the cabin entrance thinking there are three people sleeping below who will never know what hit us. Praying is an excellent idea so I offer a benediction as the tanker's klaxon begins to blast. The sound is intense, almost knocking me off my feet. We're so close I can hear the great rumble of engines from her belly accompanied by a scratchy baritone growl, a terrifying death knell signalling the end of time itself. This awful sound becomes louder and still louder as a gargantuan amount of water is pounded and jostled around the massive hull slicing its way towards us. At the last possible second, Mark puts Bagatelle's throttle to the stops and cranks her wheel to port. We spin about in the water on our beam and the giant tanker passes us within less than our boat-length! Her colossal wake follows soon after and we pitch about in the angry froth as the hulking mass moves off into the black night. Seconds later, the ship's captain is on the radio cursing up a blue streak in French and telling us we came "close to being at the bottom of the effin' river!" Québec Traffic voices their displeasure as well and demands we check in with them at regular points in the future. Rules of the road state we should have both altered starboard which is why everyone was upset with us.

We're back on our own, alone in the inky blackness. After bringing Bagatelle's engine back down from her frenzied and high-pitched whine, Mark sits at the wheel and stares transfixed at nothing. He's mouthing "Holy Shit, Holy Shit" over-and-over; I offer to take the wheel and give him time to collect his nerves. We decide to wait until late morning before breaking the news to Don. All around us the air is cold, quiet and I'm aware of a dim light on the eastern horizon as dawn begins to show itself.

Dawn beginning to break, Eric at the helm. Several NM away from our run-in with the tanker.

Despite the excitement it doesn't take long for both Mark and I to get a well-deserved rest when we come off watch. Awakening just after lunch we find Bagatelle in the large expanse of water between Québec City and Lévis. The day is bright and sunny as we motor through the bustling water-way. The city-scape on our starboard side is magnificent! Ferries make their way across the channel while pleasure boats of all shapes and sizes zoom past us.

14h10: arrive at Yacht Club de Québec (YCdQ).

We head into town for supper; I've worked up an enormous appetite from this morning so the food is terrific when it arrives. Arriving at Chez Dagobert later, we run into a classmate who's staying at a youth hostel with seven (seven!) attractive European ladies. The night is good to us and we end up taking a cab back to the Yacht Club in order to be ready to leave at 02h30 with the tide. A gale moves in so we end up staying put for the night.

Bagatelle and crew enroute to Yacht Club de Québec. Château Frontenac can be seen in the background.

## 20 August 2001, Québec to Batiscan

Strong winds persist throughout the day as we wait for the tides to turn. Don indicates he'll feel much more comfortable if we fly both the storm jib and main. We locate the storm jib without any trouble but it takes a few minutes of rummaging through the forward lockers to locate the storm main. I'm caught off guard by how small its sail bag is! The jib is designed to keep a boat stable and pointed in very high winds while the main helps the boat make progress towards safe harbour. These sails are designed to be quick to put up and take down as needed. Everyone checks their wet-weather gear to ensure it is all in one piece and accessible at a moment's notice. Topside, we get Bagatelle's sails and rigging ready before leaving the Yacht Club.

15h46: leave YCdQ.

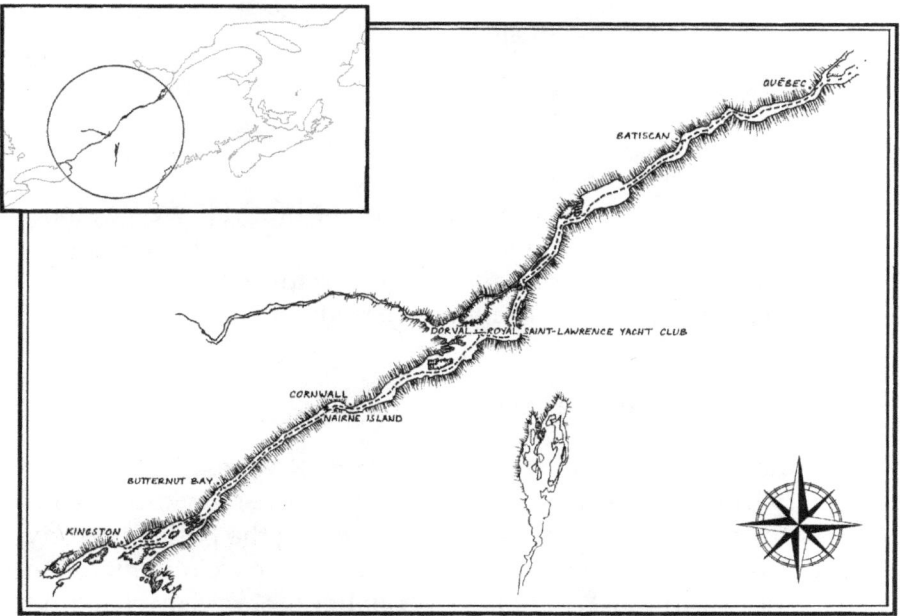

The last portion of Bagatelle's return to Kingston, ON. We proceed from Québec to Batiscan then stay one night at Montréal, QC. Heading south-west we stop Cornwall then stay at Butternut Bay followed by our arrival in Kingston, ON.

Once out in the St Lawrence Don signals us to raise the storm sails. I admit I'm a bit skeptical as these are mere postage stamps compared to the others! I'm soon humbled: once past the sanctity of Québec city we discover the gale remains in full swing along the unprotected stretch of river before us. Aided by the incoming rush of tides, we're making a good 8 to 8 1/2 kt with 31 kt apparent wind. Dan manages to take a very blurry photo of me at the helm, I'm running Bagatelle's rudder from one end to the other as we careen our way through the crashing waves. Now this is sailing!

## 21 August 2001, Batiscan to Royal St Lawrence Yacht Club

00h03: anchor at Batiscan anchorage.

07h05: leave Batiscan anchorage.

12h02: arrive Trois-Rivières Marina.

We're under a slight rain as we arrive at the marina. We stay long enough to replenish fuel plus water and get food while docked. "The Cat" passed us earlier today, moving fast on our port-side. She is a ferry on hydrofoils and carries passengers up and down the St. Lawrence Seaway.

13h00: slip Trois-Rivières Marina.

Still under cloud as we depart from Trois-Rivières. I get supper underway mid-afternoon as we're going to have roast turkey with all of the trimmings. I'm down below getting the potatoes ready with several folks topside when Mike calls out a freighter moving up on our stern. She's making good on her progress up river and will soon overtake us. As distance closes our crew are aware this is a super freighter, twice as long as any we've encountered on our trip! She's off our port beam in no time and passing us. Dan alerts everyone to her massive wake: no more than seconds pass before everyone below is thrown about Bagatelle's bowels as we rock through the sudden fury of waves. Thanks to Don's gimballed stove, supper is not lost.

Everyone is a bit groggy after supper after eating so much food: we take longer than usual to clean up the galley and wash dishes. I'm at the helm when there's an incredible explosion followed by cursing! Don's oven isn't shut off, leading to an accumulation of propane igniting and ripping the door open. Mark, who was the closest of all the crew to the stove when it happened, is lucky he's still in one piece! We all resolve to be more careful in checking the stove is indeed "off" in the future.

## 22 August 2001, Enroute to Montréal

04h38: Mark arises from the dead, Dan soon to get to sleep. Mike wakes up with an irate look at all the commotion. Maybe he should sleep less; it would make him more tired, thus more capable of sleeping through noise. Note: charts to the head wake people up!

09h10: come alongside at first lock. Advised we will have to wait until 10h30 to 11h00 to go through.

10h55: left Saint-Lambert Lock.

11h15: pass under Champlain Bridge.

12h19: arrive at Côte-Sainte-Catherine Lock, it's open but we're required to wait another twenty-five minutes for no valid reason. As we arrive a power boat proceeds out of the lock down-bound. No other vessels are approaching, the lock is open but we're not permitted to enter. This same sort of incident took place on upstream trip in 1996!

12h47: signal given to go through lock.

13h01: through Côte-Sainte-Catherine Lock. After waiting thirty minutes for entrance to open, the operators' excuse: it is lunch hour and then further refused to provide their names. They mention there are no longer any chief operators at the locks.

15h45: arrive at Royal St Lawrence Yacht Club at Dorval. Mike leaves by train from Dorval to get back to Kingston.

Dan, Mark and I make use of the club's pool then head for downtown Montréal. We go to the Peel Pub for dinner and end up staying out quite late. None of us are all that eager to head back to the yacht club but we all know Don will be very upset if his entire crew isn't back and ready in time to set sail the following morning.

## 23 August 2001, Royal St Lawrence Yacht Club to Cornwall

08h33: slip Royal St Lawrence Yacht Club.

Dan and Bagatelle silhouetted by the setting sun on one of our final days of sailing before making Kingston.

14h54: arrive at Saint-Louis Bridge #9, they wait until we are within feet of the bridge before responding to our horn.

I don't understand why we receive shoddy treatment at each lock and bridge during our voyage through Québec; it might be due to our run-in with the tanker. Or it could simply be that the lock and bridge operators have a general dislike for smaller vessels.

16h11: arrive Salaberry-de-Valleyfield Bridge #10, another vessel already waiting.

16h40: make way through bridge.

19h50: red sunset photographed by Eric.

20h22: Canadian Prospector shines a big-ass light on us!

We point Don's biggest flashlight on our main to signal to the other ship we're a sailboat. Everyone aboard Bagatelle is annoyed when the ship directs its spot-light on us, wiping out all of our night vision. I'm thinking they are not taking any chances and making good and sure we see them as much as they see us.

## 24 August 2001, at Cornwall

00h12: arrive in Cornwall at public wharf.

Everyone enjoys their time in Cornwall, we stay with Mark's parents. Everyone has an awesome lunch made by Mark's mother.

## 24 August 2001, Cornwall to Nairne Island

14h40: slip Cornwall with Guy (Mark's father) aboard.

19h20: arrive, drop anchor at Nairne Island in 21 ft of water.

After supper, Mark, Dan and Don take Baguette to shore. They are gone for a long while! Upon return we find out they've visited a number of campsites. Mark tells us he's moved one of the picnic coolers on one of the campers and someone calls out from a tent: "maybe it's raccoons! Check the trees!" A flashlight shines up as the three hide in bushes. Dan and I make our way to shore. We leopard crawl up to the campsite, set up a small tee-pee of sparklers away from anything combustible and then try to ignite them with a BBQ lighter. They take forever to catch; I'm unaware Dan has left and is making a run for it as he hears the rustle of sleeping bags and zippers. I get back on my feet and go into a flat run: Dan is tripping over picnic tables as we rush back to shore. Looking over my shoulder the car, tent and entire campsite is as bright as day. Arriving back on the boat, Don wonders if those people ever got back to sleep.

## 25 August 2001, Nairne Island to Butternut Bay

08h47: slipped.

22h30: arrive and drop anchor at Butternut Bay in 34 ft of water.

## 26 August 2001, Butternut Bay to Kingston

07h30: weigh anchor.

15h30: arrive home at Kingston Yacht Club (KYC), wind 24 kt from the south-west.

## Afterward

Our last few days of sailing are enjoyable as we make our way through the Thousand Islands. Passing under bridges between USA and Canada is interesting and there's lots of scenery along both shores. We pass by Boldt Castle in the morning and wonder how long it took to build. We're under sail as we hit the eastern portion of Wolfe Island, winds have picked up and it doesn't take us long to reach Point Fredrick. The skies are overcast as we arrive at KYC: crew depart after thanking Don for an amazing voyage. We turn our attention to the upcoming semester; little do I know this trip is the inception of my desire for more and more sailing, with many excursions to come.

| Depart | Arrive | Accum Time on Boat [days] | Accum Time Underway [hours] | Accum Engine Time [hours] | Accum Distance [NM] | Average Speed [kt] |
|---|---|---|---|---|---|---|
| Halifax | Sheet Harbour | 1 | 18.5 | 4.6 | 64.3 | 3.5 |
| Sheet Harbour | Liscombe Harbour | 2 | 27.6 | Not available | 103.7 | 4.3 |
| Liscombe Harbour | Whitehead Harbour | 3 | 36.5 | 10.4 | 156.0 | 5.9 |
| Whitehead Harbour | Canso | 4 | 41.1 | 15.2 | 178.7 | 4.9 |
| Canso | Port Hawkesbury | 5 | 45.8 | 20.1 | 204.6 | 5.6 |
| Port Hawkesbury | D'Escousse | 5 | 51.8 | 22.7 | 227.1 | 3.7 |
| D'Escousse | St Peter's | 6 | 53.3 | 24.0 | 233.0 | 4.0 |
| St Peter's | Corbett's Cove | 6 | 53.9 | Not available | 234.9 | 2.8 |
| Corbett's Cove | Dundee | 7 | 58.9 | 25.7 | 254.2 | 3.9 |
| Dundee | St Peter's | 7 | 63.1 | 27.4 | 275.3 | 5.1 |
| St Peter's | Port Hawkesbury | 8 | 70.1 | 33.3 | 301.8 | 3.8 |
| Port Hawkesbury | Charlottetown | 10 | 89.2 | 44.1 | 395.7 | 4.9 |
| Charlottetown | Îles-de-la-Madeleine | 12 | 116.8 | 52.6 | 539.4 | 5.2 |
| Îles-de-la-Madeleine | Gaspé | 14 | 150.6 | 63.8 | 711.1 | 5.1 |
| Gaspé | Matane | 17 | 196.2 | Not available | 893.6 | 4.0 |
| Matane | Rimouski | 17 | 204.6 | 93.3 | 942.4 | 5.8 |
| Rimouski | Tadoussac | 18 | 218.6 | 105.7 | 998.1 | 4.0 |
| Tadoussac | Cap-à-l'Aigle | 19 | 228.8 | 113.6 | 1,035.3 | 3.7 |
| Cap-à-l'Aigle | Québec | 19 | 244.6 | 126.2 | 1,110.9 | 4.8 |
| Québec | Batiscan | 21 | 252.9 | 127.7 | 1,157.9 | 5.7 |
| Batiscan | Royal St Lawrence Yacht Club | 22 | 285.6 | 155.8 | 1,259.9 | 3.1 |
| Royal St Lawrence Yacht Club | Cornwall | 24 | 301.2 | 170.3 | 1,310.7 | 3.2 |
| Cornwall | Nairne Island | 24 | 305.9 | 174.9 | 1,324.9 | 3.0 |
| Nairne Island | Butternut Bay | 26 | 319.6 | 184.8 | 1,368.1 | 3.1 |
| Butternut Bay | Kingston | 26 | 327.6 | 187.6 | 1,405.7 | 4.7 |

Engine Time vs Time Underway  57.3%

Time Underway vs Time on Boat  52.5%

Table 1. Trip summary for Bagatelle's return voyage from Halifax, NS to Kingston, ON in 2001.

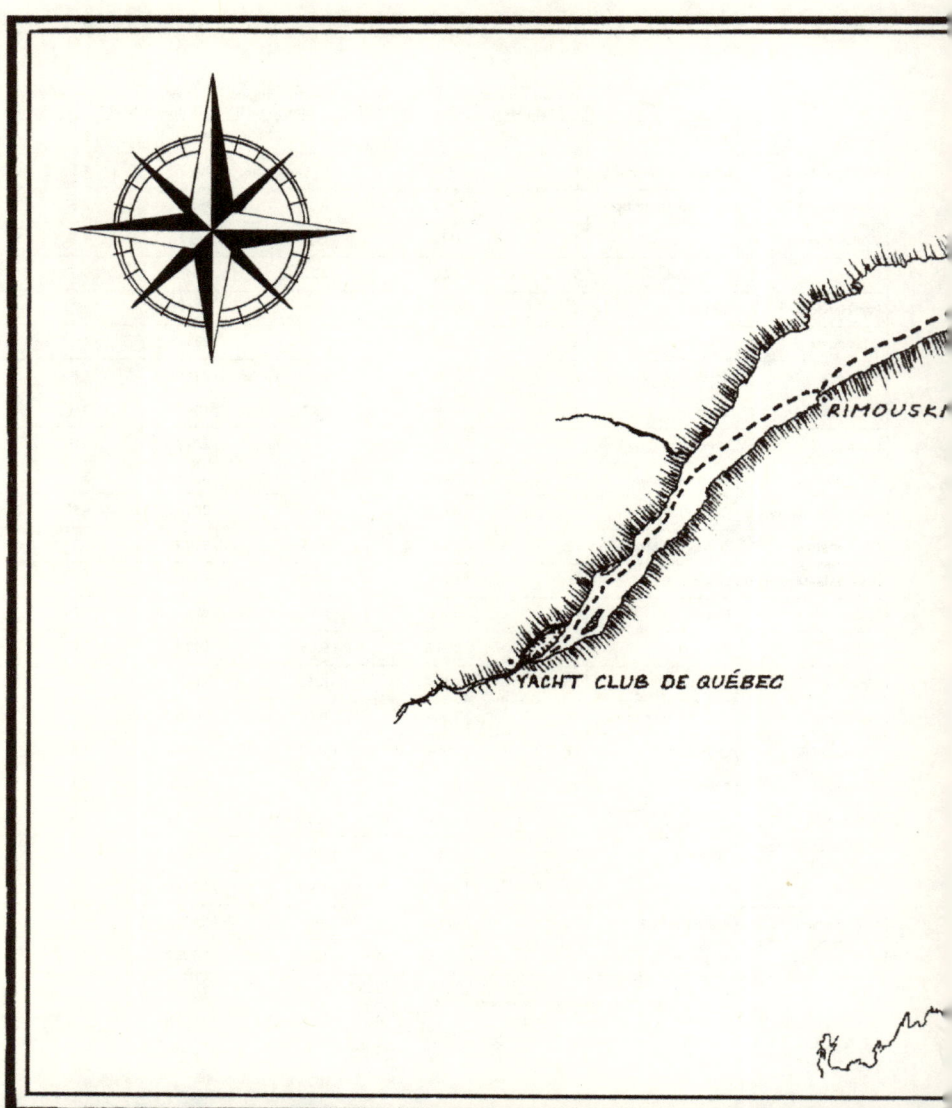

Chapter 2

*Québec, QC to Baddeck, NS*

**16 to 29 July 2003**

Summer is here and I'm getting ready to head for North Sydney, Cape Breton to join Bagatelle. I make contact with Don on his cell phone a few days before the start of my trip. He tells me the boat is stuck in Québec with engine trouble; I'll have to re-schedule my flight. A quick call to Air Canada and my flights are re-booked. It is a long series of flights from Edmonton, AB to Québec, QB although I arrive at a decent time in the afternoon with an overcast sky. Once at the yacht club I get a better appreciation of what the Skipper and crew have been up to these past few weeks. Don is frustrated as he, the boat and crew are stranded until several parts and a mechanic arrive to repair the errant engine. The person I'm replacing has already left: his entire trip was spent aboard the boat while she's docked in Québec! Andrew, a fellow crewman, waits with Don and makes a few entries in the boat's log during the weeks the boat is out of the water for repairs.

## 16 July 2003, At YCdQ

16h00: Don says we must do something to improve morale so we do "make and mend," whipping the ends of the sheets and lines. "The beatings will continue until morale improves." Reason for low morale: UPS could not find mechanics to deliver parts ergo... We are here until at least tomorrow if not Thursday.

17h00: Eric arrives.

22h00: we're still here, transmission NOT included. Still no repairs completed, maybe tomorrow.

## 17 July 2003, YCdQ to Rimouski

Not wanting to sit around the Yacht Club all day, I make my way into the city for sight-seeing. I ask the person at the reception desk for the best way of getting down-town. She tells me the club has bikes that can be borrowed free-of-charge for patrons. Don just about has a bird when he finds out they could have ridden bikes for free while they were stranded here!

I'm soon on one of the gratis bikes and making my way into the heart of the city. Old Québec captures one's heart and soul, be they passer-by or long-time resident. A large effort is underway in this city for the preservation of Francophone culture and tradition spanning hundreds of years. Old Québec boasts everything historic and authentic from gas lamps to wood fireplaces to cobble-stone streets. It is something one needs to experience first-hand: I'm glad I'm once again able to walk its streets and eat awesome food from so many restaurants, bakeries and shops.

17h08: transmission replaced by Normand Lepage Méchanautique Inc. Cost to install: $517.50, cost of parts from Anthony Keats: $594.43, cost of haul-out: $531.42.

18h30: charting program is up-and-running, sails are ready. We leave in less than two hours, hot-to-trot!

20h30: Don, Andrew and Eric leave YCdQ under sail in a thunderstorm of short duration with one reef in main and working jib. Wow, the day arrives at last.

## 18 July 2003, Enroute to Rimouski

There is little light in this dark night as we head down river towards the mouth of the St Lawrence. I'm at the helm and spot a buoy off our starboard bow, about 1 NM ahead of us. Attention is drawn away for a few moments and then it passes us a little too close for comfort: I need to make more effort to keep watching forward.

01h40: abreast of K103... Made contact with starboard aft section... Damn. Currents too strong.

Seated at the chart table, I'm fighting off drowsiness. Don is asleep when Andrew blurts out we're going to make contact with a buoy. We hit it with a tremendous bang and I'm thrown to the floor! Moments later I notice a large crack has formed in the galley counter-top. The commotion is enough to wake Don up and we head top-side to check with Andrew. There's not much to see in the murky darkness that surrounds us and after a quick check of Bagatelle's interior we determine there isn't any ingress of water. Don finds out later that the cost of repairs to Bagatelle's hull are in excess of $1000.00. It is the prudent thing to do, considering the boat is at sea for protacted periods of time!

13h24: sunny but cold! Using forward fuel tank since YCdQ and down to 3/4 gauge.

14h44: Andrew has a seawater shower, quite brisk!

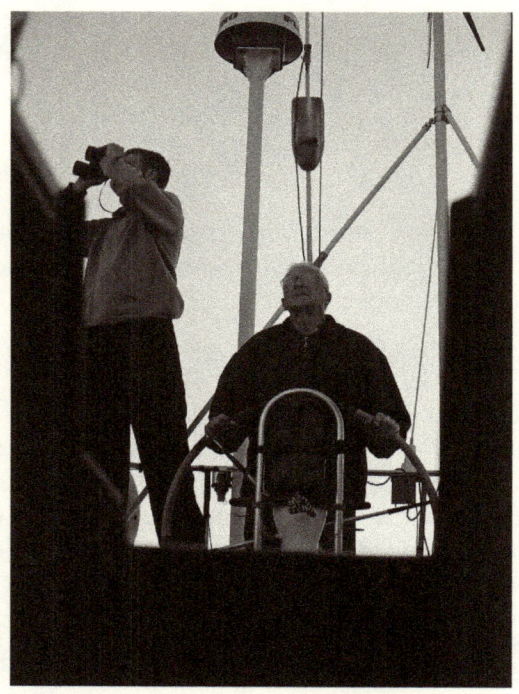

Don and Andrew on watch for more errant buoys somewhere between Matane and Rimouski.

Andrew is an experienced sailor and being in the Navy has its advantages on a trip like this. He's much more accustomed to the somewhat austere conditions of life at sea. The afternoon is cool and there's a slight rain when he announces to Don and I that it's time for his bath. He is at a point of revelry as he brings Don's mop bucket up from Bagatelle's bowels and moves forward to her heaving pulpit. Attached to a cord the bucket gets dunked into the icy cold of the St Lawrence and brought back up on deck. I cringe a bit and think that we're not that far away from our next stop, at one point I even make the suggestion to wait until Rimouski but Andrew is not having any of it. I begin to get the impression that this is a "check in the box" for his trip.

19h30: close to Rimouski after a great steak dinner by Andrew. Cool but sunny and clear, a long way to motor from Sillery on forward tank.

20h45: secure at Rimouski, forward tank 1/4 full.

Andrew walks up the starboard spreaders on a dare as we make our way eastward.

## 19 July 2003, Rimouski to Summerside

We fuel prior to departure: 34.2L in Bagatelle's forward tank, 34.5L in aft. The amount of fuel consumed between Québec and Rimouski is due to little wind since the start of this portion of Bagatelle's trip in addition to no stops in-between.

09h40: slipped Rimouski.

11h25: Groupe C.T.M.A. passenger steamer comes up alongside to inspect us at close quarters. They're from Île du Cap-aux-Meules. Andrew moons them.

11h44: protected wreck close by 48°37.5'N, 68°24.5'W, SoG 5.9 kt. White buoy on protected wreck with yellow light and MCC Québec Coast Guard ERE, three small vessels south of it.

18h57: alongside Bell Mo(A) by Matane.

It takes quite a long time to prepare supper tonight: we're having penne with Italian sausage. Don doesn't agree with this meal and is quite upset at how long it takes to prepare. Refer to my comment about garlic on p.2. The quantity of dirty dishes is also a point of contention: Don is delegated with galley clean-up tonight and his level of agitation is growing worse with each dirty pot and pan. On the days when Don cooks supper, he prides himself in using as few dishes as possible. His frustration continues to mount and once back up at the wheel, he blurts out "where's my ****ing dessert?!" I reach for the cookies although I think everyone is disappointed we're not having pie or something more substantial to help quell the taste of supper. I need to do a better job picking out groceries for this trip!

23h39: Don figures out we've changed time zones.

## 20 July 2003, Enroute to Summerside

Being three on a boat this size means a minimum of two people must be on watch at night and in nasty weather. Rough waters often cause large and uncomfortable rocking action and result in very little rest for crew off-watch. We each take four-hour breaks between watches, with one person rotating onto the "dog-watch"[2] every few iterations. Given we are still at the beginning of our trip, I'm not as concerned when I get less than an ideal amount of sleep. However, this is rather insidious as the lack of sleep becomes cumulative over a number of days while we're at sea with no respite. Having four hours of rest doesn't mean much since it takes me a considerable time to fall asleep. My rest is often interrupted due to the wave action, noise from Bagatelle's engine and a myriad number of strong smells within her cabin. Don puts coffee on during his watch and it's enough to keep anyone awake by getting a slight whiff.

01h40: Eric at wheel, stars out and phosphorescent plankton are lighting up as we pass by. This is what sailing is all about.

Night sailing with clear sky on the open ocean is every bit as enjoyable as it sounds. Alone in the sea the boat rocks and sways through the water with the rustle of rigging and a subtle, gentle hiss of the waves against her sides. Far removed from the developed world my view is clear: a stunning display of the cosmos with no interruption from artificial light apart from the dim glow of Bagatelle's navigation and compass lights. Parts of the trip are on the open water with no land in sight, with a complete openness to the sky. Still other portions are in view of land, with lights on-shore piercing through the darkness.

05h22: pass Sainte-Anne-des-Monts.

12h30: abeam of Cap-de-la-Madeleine. Sea flat, overcast, no wind.

18h30: alongside Saint-Maurice-de-l'Échouerie.

18h53: thunderstorm a'brew'n to starboard matey, arr!

19h10: sails down.

---

[2] A dog watch, in marine or naval terminology, is a period of work duty between 16h00 and 20h00. This period is split into two, with the 'first' dog watch from 16h00 to 18h00 and the 'last' dog watch from 18h00 to 20h00. Each of these watches is half the length of a standard watch. The definition in this foot-note is licensed under a Creative Commons Attribution 3.0 License, original work copyright Wikipedia®: Dog Watch, http://en.wikipedia.org/wiki/Dog_watch, February 2015.

19h39: secured Rivière-au-Renard.  Forward tank almost empty, switch to aft.  We get water, no stores are open so we leave.

20h45: out of Rivière-au-Renard, on course for Summerside.  Under sail for a change!

## 21 July 2003, Enroute to Summerside

Night turns to dawn as we punch through the waves with a steady south-west wind. The day is overcast and we make good time in the morning. Towards afternoon, the winds begin to weaken and our speed bleeds off. Thinking about our level of provisions for the remainder of our trip I decide to make Shepherd's Pie tonight, using stores kept aboard Bagatelle from the days of yore. It turns out to be half-decent and everyone is glad that there will be leftovers for lunch the following day.

19h00: under sail and engine as SoG is 2 kt and we have about 112 NM to go!

22h45: we reefed the main Ye Hearties!

23h05: tacked on a port tack.

Winds have come back and as I make my way topside to start my watch I'm aware we're moving quite fast. Andrew tells me about the conditions we're sailing in: on our present tack and with sails trimmed, he doesn't have to put a lot of effort into keeping Bagatelle pointed into the wind. In fact, we're rocketing through the waves with almost no impediment. She's in her element at this part of the trip, her mast is singing. This is much more enjoyable sailing from what we encountered earlier on this leg!

## 22 July 2003, Enroute to Summerside

03h45: 47°27.24'N, 64°34.13'W, 7.9kt, 170° magnetic (M). Where's the f******* pen?  Tacked, headed for the Strait of Northumberland.

06h54: frustrating - getting nowhere!  Raining too.  With working jib and one reef in main we are not putting well at all, and a number of leaks make life miserable for all.

Top-side at the break of dawn I'm engulfed in the scent of the ocean, all calm and primordial. I move forward to catch the wave action at the pulpit. Perched on the highest rung with my back against the cold steel of the forestay, I begin to smell land. We're another hour away before coming within view of the north-western tip of PEI but there's land there, I know it! We end up coming close, close enough to see every blade of the massive wind farm on this part of the island. Altering to starboard, we make our way westward as the wind is in the exact direction where we want to head. Those who've sailed up-wind will empathize with our plight: tacking on either a port or starboard tack in these conditions leaves us on a heading that is well-removed from our desired course.

11h57: chart program is down, computer might be too hot.

Out into the Northumberland Strait, the waves pick up and we're now rolling though substantial swells! With Andrew down below preparing supper, I'm at the helm and enjoying the thrill of Bagatelle cresting each massive wave, plunging down the other side and putting everything forward of her anchor into the water. This is of course rather upsetting to the crew down below; Andrew is flying through the cabin as we reach the extreme of each wave, so I take us through a few of these before I decide to ease up. Supper is soon over as we're all a bit on edge with yet another approaching storm.

23h20: there is a lot of wind and a night arrival is not attractive with a double reef in the main in addition to a thunderstorm warning.

01h07: two successive tacks to wait out the wind appear to have worked. Wind is now 17 kt.

Night is soon upon us as I get my head down before the next watch. We're making for the harbour entrance and sure to make Summerside while I'm asleep. I'm looking forward to making use of a functioning toilet, one that doesn't feel like a shoddy amusement park ride combined with an arcane hazing ritual. To make matters worse, we're running low on food and water at this point in our trip due to lack of replenishment at our last stop. As

I come up on watch, I can't be sure at first as to where we're headed but something tells me we're moving away from our destination, not towards it! Don informs us of the need to tack back-and-forth and wait the storm out until we can make for the safety of Summerside. The entrance is too difficult, coupled with little to no visibility at night for us to make in this rough weather. We await the arrival of dawn, frustration building all the while. I'm on my last nerve from having every berth soaked from various leaks, being constipated beyond belief and tired as Hell from jostling through the rough seas we've encountered these past few days. At long last, dawn breaks and the weather calms down. We make for Summerside, having a number of now-visible points to navigate about to get through a narrow channel leading to the marina. Everyone is quick to secure Bagatelle and then get heads down for a well-deserved rest!

## 23 July 2003, Summerside to Charlottetown

08h30: secure at Summerside, 36.7L in fwd tank, 17.5L into aft tank.

After a few hours' sleep we make our way into town to stock up on food. The Yacht Club is well cared for and there are a number of shops along the boardwalk making the place quite attractive for passers by. Once in the grocery store I'm struck by the amount of confectionery and junk food; there are number of aisles dedicated to it. We resist temptation to load up on sweets and comfort food despite all the challenges from the past few days. Pretty soon we're back at the Yacht Club and making ready to cast off for Charlottetown.

13h24: left Summerside harbour and Yacht Club provisioned, clean and having clean laundry.

15h15: passed under the PEI Bridge.

A harbour seal comes up alongside to investigate Bagatelle and remains on our stern as we approach Confederation bridge; I'm sure he's wondering if we have a few fish for him. The bridge is impressive at a distance and grows larger and larger still as we sail southward. Passing underneath everyone can't help but marvel at this feat of architecture and construction engineering!

Approaching Confederation Bridge under full sail.

Andrew works the tall-boy in an effort to squeeze an extra knot out of Bagatelle.

With the bridge behind us, Andrew is keen to try one of Don's less-used sails as we make our way towards Charlottetown. He brings a tall-boy up on deck and we set about making it fast to one of the cleats forward of the main. Taking one of Don's extra halyards, the sail is soon hoisted but it doesn't seem to be flying right. I get a quick lesson in terminology as we make our adjustments to the sail. Andrew explains that the head is at the top while the tack is used to secure the lower portion, kind of like "tacking" or "nailing" it down. The clew is the point out at the far aft end, along the bottom of a sail because according to Andrew "it doesn't have a clue." He fiddles some more and attempts to secure the errant sail at various points in order to catch the best part of the slight breeze we find ourselves in. We decide to lower it as it doesn't appear to add any value.

21h48: alongside Charlottetown Yacht Club, Chinese food for supper!

I'm not caught up on my sleep so am somewhat delirious as we wait in the restaurant for supper. Making my way to the bathroom, I have hallucinations of using the head on Bagatelle and can swear the room is at a sharp slant. A noisy ventilation fan reminds me of the throb of her engine. Is that water I feel dripping on my head?

Back aboard the boat we're all looking forward to some decent and well-deserved rest. Don rummages for a few minutes and produces a large forced-air heater in a box, sheathed in a black plastic garbage bag. The heater helps take the chill out of the air although at this point I'm ecstatic for two things: one, to be docked for the night and two, sleeping quarters that haven't been subjected to a steady ingress of rain and sea-water.

Sleeping while docked is one of the more pleasant aspects of our trips as the boat is never at rest but constantly rocking and swaying with the tide and slight eddies in the shelter of the marina. For those who've spent time aboard boats you might agree with me when I say that spending the first night back on dry land in a bed that doesn't move whatsoever takes some getting used to.

## 24 July 2003, Charlottetown to Port Hawkesbury

12h50: touched bottom while trying to leave from fuel dock.

22h53: under sail again, thank gosh. Popcorn snack.

Bagatelle's draft is 6 feet, 9 inches. There are a number of times throughout our trips where we encounter trouble on account of shallow water. Don's echo sounder is in use on a regular basis when coming into docks, anchoring points, navigating through narrow channels and other constraining locations. There are two display units aboard the boat. The first is quite ancient but very reliable and is situated port-side on Bagatelle's interior and beside the ladder leading into the cabin. A second unit is located beside the helm and is equipped with a speaker to call out various depths. As we touch bottom leaving the fuel dock at Charlottetown, I'm reminded of our last trip when Mark joked about the depth sounder, saying it should call out "you're... f***ed" when the keel is about to touch bottom.

Once we're out on the open water I set about making us popcorn. Don's stove, while dependable, requires an element of patience to operate: each of the three burners needs to be tended with loving care. Don's "toaster" sits atop of one of the burners and you have to be quick to flip pieces of bread before they burn. One of my top priorities on each trip aboard Bagatelle is ensuring the crew get as many decent meals as possible. While breakfast and lunch can be cold, we all make an effort to have hot food for supper regardless of the weather. I'm happy preparing most meals as it means I have more control over what we eat, but there are times when I welcome other people anteing up with cooking.

## 25 July 2003, Enroute to Port Hawkesbury

01h55: after a sudden wind increase we round Cape George and put in a single reef as we are over-powered.

06h15: pass through Canso Locks.

07h00: secure at Port Hawkesbury.

18h30: Andrew leaves for Halifax to fly back home.

## 26 July 2003, At Port Hawkesbury

1900: Kim arrives to join Bagatelle as an incoming crewman.

Don, Kim and I head into town to "Billy Joe's" for a few drinks. Don and Kim make their way back to Bagatelle around 01h00; I stay for a while longer. The rest of the night seems to pass by quickly and there's a bit of rain as I make my way back aboard Bagatelle around 6:00 AM the next day.

A photo of us docked at St Peter's Canal, waiting for the locks to open.

## 27 July 2003, Port Hawkesbury to St Peter's

11h50: Don, Andrew, Eric and Kim slipped Port Hawkesbury.

14h55: pass by MacDonald Shoal.

There are several places to dock and anchor at Baddeck; in addition, it boasts a generous marine hardware store.

With a proclivity to change its mind at any moment, weather in the Maritimes is a source of constant worry, bemusement and bewilderment for boaters. Don is seasoned at checking MAFORs (marine forecasts) over VHF and applies a bit of religious fervour in doing so. More than once this practice is appreciated by crew as we can at least prepare the boat and her sails for a sudden onset of worsening wind, wave and anything else the weather brings. Also more than once, crew have missed opportunities to keep apprised of changes in weather while the Skipper is off-watch or otherwise indisposed, to everyone's detriment.

15h10: take down sails to go through Lennox Passage.

15h48: pass under Lennox Bridge, we will become part of some person's holiday video footage for sure.

18h10: moor at locks at St Peter's.

## 28 July 2003, St Peter's to Baddeck

09h29: being lowered in locks at St Peter's.

13h50: cross Barra Strait Bridge in heavy winds after taking down sails in 25 kt winds.

The winds take us by surprise as we move beyond the safety of the strait. Don gives the order to down sails since we don't have the right weight for this wind and we are close enough to motor to Baddeck. The jib is difficult to lower as winds are gusting well beyond safe limits for this amount of sail! Everyone is working as we head up into the wind. Without warning the jib sheets are let loose. Crew have to wrestle with a huge sail in this rough wind: I'm fighting to get one of the sheets under control when a loose end comes screaming through the air and smacks me square in the face. Don remarks later he's never heard anyone curse like that.

16h00: secure at Baddeck.

20h00: Trevor arrives to assume crew duties as Eric prepares to depart.

## 29 July 2003, At Baddeck

Crew head into town for a day of sight-seeing. We visit the Alexander Graham Bell Museum with several interesting artifacts and drawings. Baddeck comes alive in the summertime: the population grows on account of tourism. There are numerous places for boats to dock and anchor. Shops bustle with people coming and going. Despite an influx of people, the town maintains a quaint and peaceful atmosphere. Situated along a pristine estuary and nestled in rolling hills it is easy to see why many people identify this part of Canada's geography as similar to Scotland.

15h45: Eric departs.

## Afterward

Having no means of transportation to return to Halifax and a plane headed home, I quickly strike a deal with Trevor. He needs someone to return his car to Port Hawkesbury and I need to get myself to a place with steady bus service. Driving along the winding roads I can't help but notice the large number of police cars out-and-about. Making Port Hawkesbury I park the car at the bus terminal, spend a few moments in town and board the evening bus to Halifax. Reflecting on the past few days I'm in awe of the rough weather we encounter in the Northumberland Strait as we make Summerside. Canada's waters have a tremendous potential for challenge and adventure to all who set sail upon them!

| Depart | Arrive | Accum Time on Boat [days] | Accum Time Underway [hours] | Accum Engine Time [hours] | Accum Distance [NM] | Average Speed [kt] |
|---|---|---|---|---|---|---|
| Québec | Rimouski | 1 | 24.3 | 24.0 | 160.4 | 6.6 |
| Rimouski | Rivière-au-Renard | 3 | 58.2 | 39.4 | 349.9 | 5.6 |
| Rivière-au-Renard | Summerside | 6 | 118.0 | 46.3 | 639.3 | 4.8 |
| Summerside | Charlottetown | 6 | 126.4 | 54.4 | 691.9 | 6.3 |
| Charlottetown | Port Hawkesbury | 8 | 144.5 | 62.4 | 789.6 | 5.4 |
| Port Hawkesbury | St Peter's | 10 | 150.9 | Not available | 815.8 | 4.1 |
| St Peter's | Baddeck | 11 | 157.4 | 69.7 | 845.8 | 4.6 |

Engine Time vs Time Underway 44.3%

Time Underway vs Time on Boat 59.6%

Table 2. Trip summary for Bagatelle's revised outbound voyage from Québec, QC to Baddeck, NS in 2003.

64   Knots Made Good

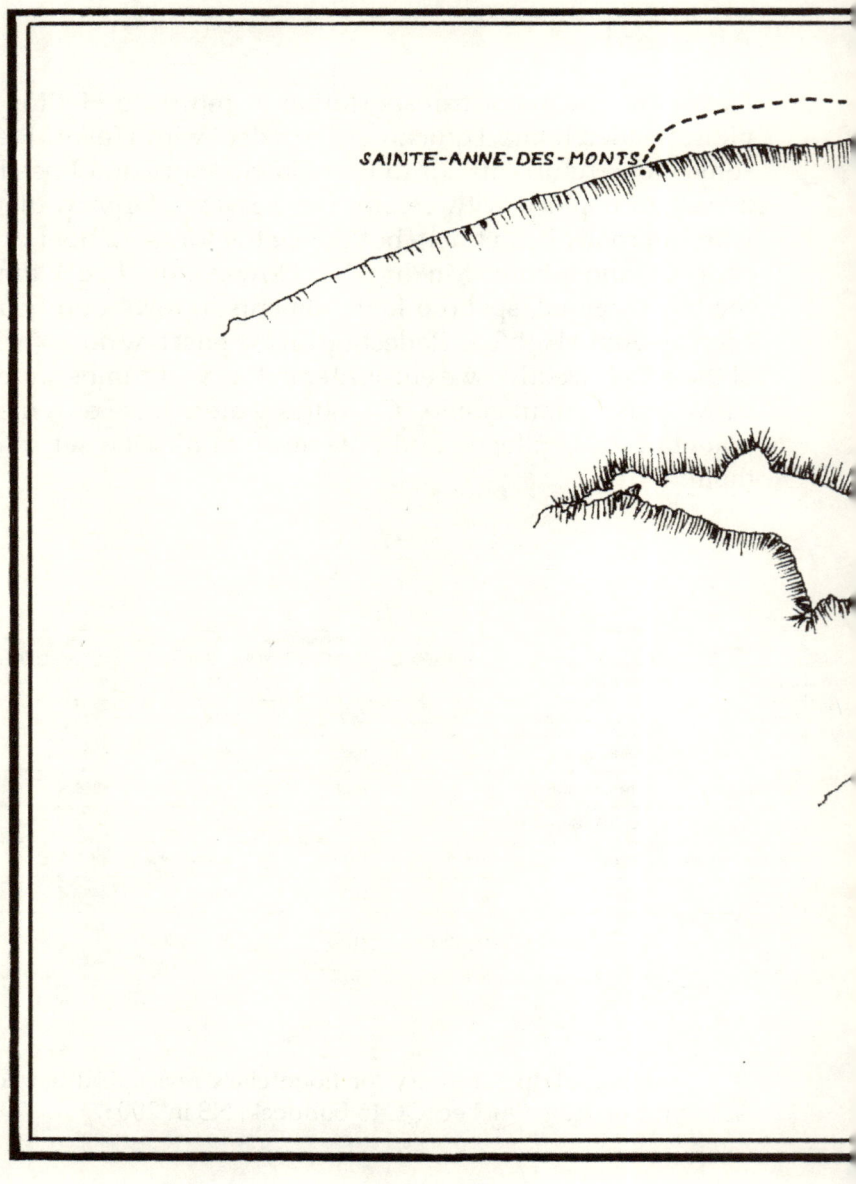

# Chapter 3

## Charlottetown, PEI to Ste Anne-des-Monts, QC

**06 to 13 August 2005**

66    Knots Made Good

East-bound and anxious to get my sea legs for the summer, I take the red-eye from Edmonton, AB to Charlottetown, PEI. Instead of being offered an aisle seat, the attendant puts me in first class! I'm so happy to have leg-room and a comfortable seat I pass on the meal being served in the morning as we make our way towards PEI. Sleep is more important at this time as I'm aware of the small amount I'll get in the coming days. Those who know how much I like eating can appreciate that I don't take this decision lightly!

## 06 August 2005, At Charlottetown

11h45: Eric arrives.

12h30: go and get Andrew who's having trouble with his phone.

We hit a grocery store in Charlottetown after meeting up with Andrew. Don asks "do you like liver?" as we make our way past the deli section. Similar to other occasions, I decline and offer to pick up chicken breasts instead. Shake-n-bake chicken, rice and corn are staples whenever I'm on the boat. My tactic is to do as much cooking as possible while I'm aboard for two reasons: one, I get to chose what we eat and two, dishes are someone else's responsibility! Food that makes its way onto the boat is seldom if ever taken back off. Myself and other crew find some interesting "science projects" on more than one occasion at the backs of some of Bagatelle's lockers. Don is determined not to let anything go to waste, never mind whether the fruits and vegetables have a slight off-color to them. I learn later that his wife Sylvia, never, never, NEVER allows "boat food" into their house.

20h00: supper at Chinese restaurant on north side of Main St.

22h00: Doug, our fourth crewman, arrives for the third time and misses us again.

## 07 August 2005, Charlottetown to Îles-de-la-Madeleine

06h30: Don, Andrew, Eric and Doug slipped.

07h00: pass lighthouse at entrance to Charlottetown.

07h40: pancakes, full of "bonus chunks" both fuzzy and green. Don needs Tupperware for stuff like pancake mix.

12h35: Don throws (empty) can of Habitant overboard. The Coast Guard will be on their way to arrest crew of Bagatelle.

Very few items can be thrown overboard: scraps of paper towel and compostable food waste are part of an exclusive list of candidates for jettison while at sea.

13h20: pass PEI ferry off stern, Doug and Andrew put on a show by mooning them.

## 08 August 2005, Enroute to Îles-de-la-Madeleine

03h05: pass fishing boat about 300m on starboard side.

04h45: Eric sick - very uncomfortable.

I'm at the wheel as dawn breaks. We're in a lumpy sea as the winds have shifted; I'm getting sicker with each passing wave. Holding onto the wheel, I lean over and hurl over the top lifeline as we make our way closer and closer to the southernmost island. Don takes over as the winds grow stronger and crew are forced topside to secure the main. We elect to take it down and with all the activity my sickness subsides as everyone wrestles with an unwieldy sail. Next to come down is the jib, although we elect to fly it until getting a bit closer to the harbour to help steady our course.

08h57: secure at Îles-de-la-Madeleine.

Following a nice lunch at the marina, the Skipper and crew decide to venture beyond the small town on Île of Cap-aux-Meules. It is afternoon, the sun has broken through cloud and weather is taking a turn for the better. After we stop for ice cream Don and Andrew decide to head back to town to finish grocery shopping. Doug and I make for a rather large hill to get a good view of the island. Passing close to a radio tower we are afforded a fantastic view indeed! Equipped with a tourist map of the island we decide to make for the west coast and continue exploring. Raspberries close to the top are a nice diversion, then we continue our trek. The trees are quite thick on descending the other side of the hill: after pushing through stubborn evergreen we pop out in a clearing used in the wintertime by cross-country skiers.

Sitting down for lunch at the marina in Cap-aux-Meules.

Making our way westward we come across a small house. As we move closer a figure appears at one of the windows. He's rather irate with us for traipsing across his lawn and he blurts out "Vous n'avez pas le droit de marcher sourtout!" If this was an English-speaking community he might have shouted "get the Hell off my lawn!" instead. Moving along and back on a paved road we are happy to be out of the bush but with all the walking we're both in need of water. A few doors down from the old-timer who cussed us out, Doug engages with some kind folks who offer us drinks. Much better treatment than the first house! Continuing westward we make the coast with a tremendous view of the Gulf of St Lawrence. Rugged cliffs with deep red faces are in stunning contrast between blue sky, water and the green of the surrounding hills. We observe several amazing out-coppings, natural bridges and other formations along the edges of the cliffs, including a magnificent elephant rock. There is a tremendous cascade of water at its base and an accompanying rumble with each crash of the waves. With every passing minute I'm getting a better idea of why people flock to the Magdallen islands all the way from Montréal each summer. Walking north-eastward along the

Elephant rock formation off Île du Cap-aux-Meules.

edges of the cliffs, we reach a blueberry patch and stop for a few minutes for replenishment.  A beach is on the other side of the small cove containing the blueberry patch; it takes a few minutes of additional walking before we're at the edge of the water.  Doug mentions he'd like to go skinny-dipping, I manage to talk him out of it in the hope of avoiding the Sûreté du Québec (police) descending on the beach and spoiling our whole trip.

We make our way up Chemin des Caps, trying to hitch-hike to make it back to the marina as it is getting on close to supper.  Nobody offers to stop and so we're left to trudge back with at least a few blisters forming.  No big deal and as we round the hill-top we're afforded one more fantastic view of the harbour and surrounding countryside.  This is one place in the Maritimes people should put on their bucket lists.

## 09 August 2005, Îles-de-la-Madeleine to Gaspé

09h45: slipped.

09h53: shut down engine, main and genoa close-hauled, course-over-ground (CoG) 166°M.

12h34: pass close to coast off Île du Havre Aubert with excellent visibility.

As we leave the shelter of the islands I'm feeling the onset of more sea-sickness, after a few moments it passes and I now have my sea-legs for the remainder of our trip. We learn of an approaching storm and decide to change the jib.  Don goes by experience in deciding what sails to fly and how many reefs to use in advance of a change in weather.  Often he'll have the boat prepared for rougher weather well before it arrives. Waiting until we are in the middle of a storm to make configuration changes to Bagatelle's sails can spell disaster if the wind and waves overtake us.  I've been aboard the boat on other trips where we waited too long to change sails and the result was heart-wrenching as we witnessed several thousand dollars of sail rent into so many small pieces from the sheer force of the wind.

Along with the jib change comes an order from the Skipper to put in a couple of reefs in the main. The wind and waves have picked up, much faster than expected! Myself and two other crew scurry forward in the crashing waves and are thrashed about. All of us struggle in getting the jib lowered, secured and the storm jib up in its place. The winds are now battering everything aboard accompanied by fierce wave action. Bagatelle's rails often plunge under, her pulpit crashing up and down. Stinging salt spray swashes and envelopes the crew as they struggle with sails and rigging. Much of this evolution needs to tended outside of the cockpit: a rather large quantity of lines, sheets and halyards make for many obstacles when moving fore and aft. There's a myriad of impinging articles on-deck! Through all of this heaving and swaying the crew dance like banshees completing their tasks, darting from one spot to the next.

## 10 August 2005, Enroute to Gaspé

02h24: the genny is dragging in the water. We have fixed it until the next change of watch.

I come off my watch late in the evening, weather no less rough than earlier. Making my way forward to relieve myself prior to heading below, I notice the jib while tied down is sagging over Bagatelle's side. Thinking it won't be an issue I head below to get my rest. When Andrew wakes me up for the start of my shift I learn he and Doug had a terrible time getting the majority of the jib out of the water. With each dip of the boat's bow it works itself free from its holdings and begins to drag in the water. The waves continue to pound: Doug struggles to bring the jib back on deck when a massive wave overtakes the boat. He's submerged, swimming above Bagatelle with his harness keeping him from going overboard. He manages to regain control of the errant jib, lashing it to the deck once Andrew is able to make his way forward to lend a hand. Later when we need to free the jib it takes quite a while to loosen all of the sail-ties; Andrew and Doug had good reason for using so many!

06h15: passed by a school of dolphins and one whale right off port bow.

After being briefed on the jib I make my way topside and am forward on the pulpit when I notice a dark, round shape making its way towards the bow. It passes in front of us and Andrew later figures it's a sleeping whale.

15h20: secure at Gaspé.

Spectacular view adjacent to the marina at Gaspé.

Arriving in the afternoon with a full sun means we get to spend a few moments enjoying Gaspé and its surrounding countryside. In the daytime it is very picturesque with several houses and larger buildings nestled along the bay and up the surrounding hills. After an excellent supper downtown, everyone agrees to hit one of the bars. I'm quick to take the staff up on their special: a pail of "Coronitas." Turns out they are quite a bit smaller than the bottles Corona comes in but hey, beer is beer.

## 11 August 2005, Gaspé to Rivière-au-Renard

20h45: Don, Andrew, Eric and Alain slipped. Doug leaves after breakfast, Alain arrives in the afternoon to replace Doug as crew.

22h10: start engine, under power.

Alain and Andrew on departure from Gaspé. Although it's August the weather is cool out on the open water!

## 12 August 2005, Enroute to Rivière-au-Renard

00h09: shut down engine, using main and storm jib.

01h22: Alain sick.

02h19: lumpy seas and no progress so engine run.

03h50: Cap-des-Rosiers at 1.2 NM.

06h30: secure at Rivière-au-Renard.

## 12 August 2005, Rivière-au-Renard to Sainte-Anne-des-Monts

14h45: slipped, proceeding under storm main and storm jib, had to use engine as well. Eric takes Bonamine in place of Gravol.

17h00: Don gets a face-full of water from centre hatch when plowing through heavy swells; woke him up and got his one dry sleeping bag wet.

17h30: a small bird joins us aboard Bagatelle. After a few moments in the cockpit he flies into the cabin, lights on Don's back and then goes up to the forward quarter. The little guy passes away during the night from exposure, exhaustion or both.

20h45: fishing vessel Myrki passes real close on port side, we think her crew wanted to say "hi."

20h58: weather the sh**s, lost satellite reception.

## 13 August 2005, Enroute to Sainte-Anne-des-Monts

We're making the last few miles of my portion of this trip, the skies have cleared somewhat as we make our approach to Sainte-Anne-des-Monts. The incoming crew are waiting for us as we arrive at the marina; Mark and Tara are going to join Bagatelle for next few days. Stephen is there as well although he won't be joining the Skipper and crew on this part of the journey. Everyone on this part of the trip will have a wedding to attend once they arrive in Québec City.

12h54: secure at Sainte-Anne-des-Monts. Mark and Stephen lift up their shirts to greet us as we come up alongside the large concrete wall of the marina. Tara, Mark's significant other, just waves.

## Afterward

Before departing, Don and I explore a Marine Science Centre as the new crew get ready to leave in Bagatelle. Sainte-Anne-des-Monts has a number of interesting buildings including an old church, someday I'll be back to spend more time exploring.

| Depart | Arrive | Accum Time on Boat [days] | Accum Time Underway [hours] | Accum Engine Time [hours] | Accum Distance [NM] | Average Speed [kt] |
|---|---|---|---|---|---|---|
| Charlottetown | Îles-de-la-Madeleine | 1 | 26.4 | 7.3 | 143.6 | 5.4 |
| Îles-de-la-Madeleine | Gaspé | 3 | 57.0 | 12.1 | 315.3 | 5.6 |
| Gaspé | Rivière-au-Renard | 5 | 66.8 | 19.8 | 356.9 | 4.3 |
| Rivière-au-Renard | Sainte-Anne-des-Monts | 6 | 88.9 | 42.1 | 453.0 | 4.3 |

Engine Time vs Time Underway  47.3%

Time Underway vs Time on Boat  61.8%

Table 3. Trip summary for Bagatelle's voyage from Charlottetown, PEI to Ste-Anne-des-Monts, QC in 2005.

## 76     Knots Made Good

# Chapter 4

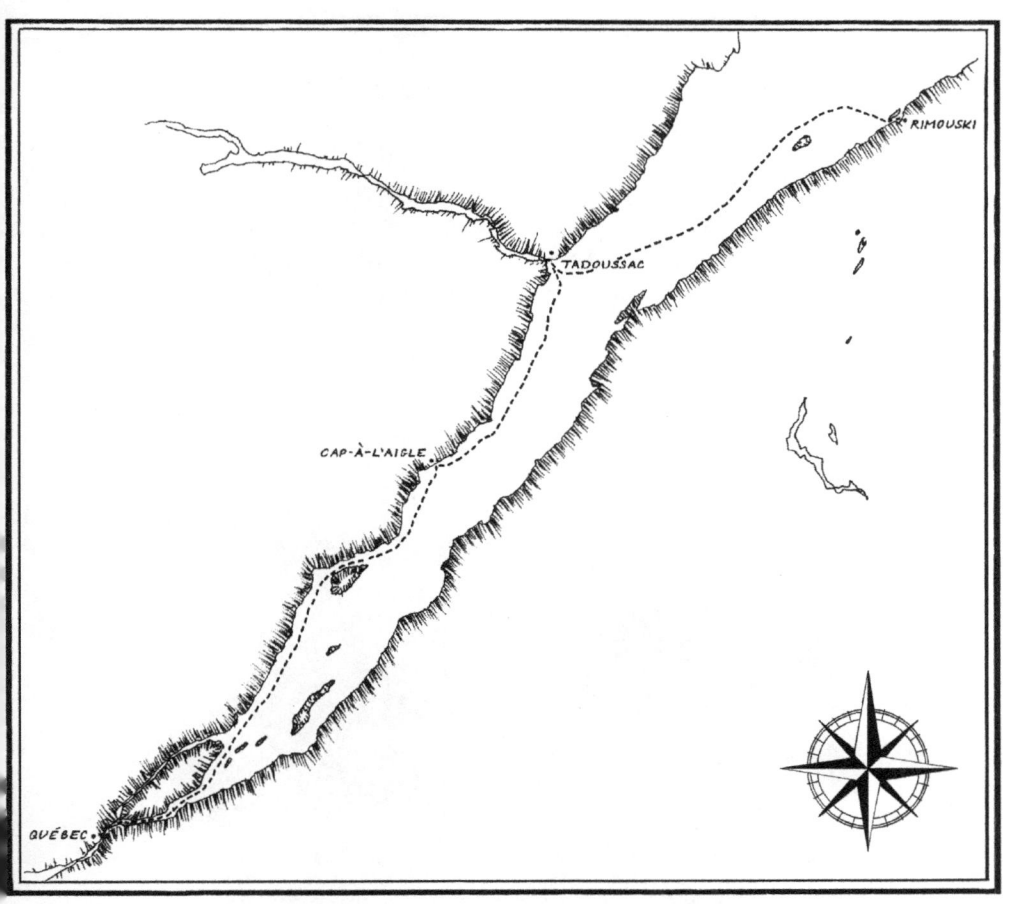

*Québec, QC to Rimouski, QC*

**27 to 30 June 2007**

Bagatelle is moored at YCdQ; it's the 27th of June and Don is waiting for Chris (his son) and I to arrive. Our plan is to swap with the other crew and make our way eastward: Arron and Paul keep Don company after completing their leg of the trip from Kingston to Québec City. Brokering a deal to ferry Arron's car, Chris leaves Kingston at the crack of dawn. He picks me up from my wife's parents in Brockville later in the morning. We make our way eastward, stopping for a quick lunch outside of Montréal. Arriving at Québec we have a few minutes for handover with Arron and Paul. Jim, our forth crewman, arrives at the same time as Chris and I. A thunderstorm develops so we end up waiting until high tide before leaving the Yacht Club. It just so happens high tide is next morning at o'dark stupid. Awesome.

The sailboat "Madcap" accompanying us down river on our departure from Québec.

## 28 June 2007, Québec to Cap-à-l'Aigle

04h12: Don, Chris, Eric and Jim depart YCdQ - cool south-west wind. Called QC traffic but they don't require our check-ins.

A fellow boater with sails down is ahead and off our port bow as we make our way east on the St Lawrence.

04h50: spoke with Madcap on radio. Their stern light is occluded by their dinghy.

Madcap is a sailboat; we meet up with her crew at the beginning of our trip and learn they are on a similar, down-bound course. They and another boat travelling with them are well-kitted out: one of the crew is blogging about their trip as they go. Our voyage from Québec to Tadoussac is shrouded in fog along several parts so we're privy to quite a bit of radio traffic between the other two boats on channel 16. It would be safer for everyone if they switched to a different one, as 16 is reserved for emergency use.

06h33: pass under hydro wires.

06h56: close to Pointe de St Laurent, SoG 6.8 kt.

11h40: freighter Canada Senator from Hamburg passing downwind to starboard 0.38 NM and we can't make out her shape, visibility poor!

12h29: pass Pte de la Prairie at Île-aux-Coudres, SoG 6.0 kt.

14h25: alongside Cap Martin, SoG 3.3 kt.

15h50: pass Cap de la Corneille.

16h00: screaming along at 0.0 kt.

18h46: arrive at Cap-à-l'Aigle.

## 29 June 2007, Cap-à-l'Aigle to Tadoussac

We are still in the first portion of Bagatelle's voyage this summer and Don is eager to make good progress. He recounts from his last trip the crew had a lot of difficulty with currents in the St Lawrence. Compounded with a thick fog and narrow passage along one portion, Skipper and crew are hard-pressed when a freighter comes up on their aft quarter and makes the passage uncomfortable for all. For the portion of the trip I'm aboard the boat, Don resolves we leave soon after midnight to catch the falling tide and use it to our advantage.

04h13: depart Cap-à-l'Aigle under power.

04h42: sun rising.

05h07: abeam of Gros Cap-à-l'Aigle, SoG 6.3 kt.

05h42: pass Point au Saumon, SoG 6.3 kt. Wind direction indicator and speedometer/log are both inoperable.

Crew look forward to their stop in Tadoussac in hope of catching a glimpse of whales and other marine life. Tadoussac is a nice stop in its own right, situated amongst several hills in a pleasant bay. This area gets a decent helping of fog: passage to and from the marina can be challenging. Don elects to approach most destinations at reduced speed, often well in advance of our arrival. This practice pays dividends in terms of safety; however, for un-seasoned crew it can be frustrating if one feels a sudden urge to make land. Upon final approach to the dock, I marvel at

Don's ability to position Bagatelle. Using a combination of forward/reverse, turns of the wheel and a gentle application of throttle Don can drive Bagatelle in any direction. Even more impressive is Don's ability to side-slip the boat towards and away from a dock along her length.

10h20: arrive Tadoussac. Distance from Tadoussac to Rimouski is 54 NM.

We have a fair amount of distance to cover to locate a grocery store; later we find one about 1/2 mile from the marina. Chris searches all over to find fishing line, upon return he discovers several rolls in Don's stores. No time left to fish as we have only a few minutes prior to cast-off and a lucky break in the fog. What few minutes we have left are spent with a quick walk along the beach close to the marina.

Bagatelle has a close run-in with a docked boat while getting fuel, winds are strong! The marina operator measures us from tip of pulpit to stern for docking fees... Don is quite upset as other marinas measure Bagatelle from the water-line. The showers cost $1.00 for every eight minutes of use.

23h15: slipped.[3]

## 30 June 2007, Tadoussac to Rimouski

05h12: sunrise 40 minutes ago.

10h25: 8.1 kt (with spinnaker up).

Since this is my last day on our trip, Don lets me take the wheel. Conditions are ideal to fly the spinnaker and we make good progress! Chris goes up forward and gets a number of decent photos perched over Bagatelle's side.

[3] Time of departure shows as "1115" in both Don's log-book and my personal notes. We spend the day in Tadoussac getting groceries and sight-seeing therefore this departure time is erroneous. In addition, looking at other trips between Rimouski and Tadoussac it takes between 10 and 14 hours. Departure time in this book is thus adjusted to read 23h15.

The wind is in our favour enroute to Rimouski from Tadoussac.

10h59: spinnaker down, 5.6 kt.

12h12: arrive at Rimouski.  Showers cost $1.00 for 8 minutes (same price as Tadoussac).  Mike, owner of Crusader, a Redline 39 offers to provide transportation for groceries.

We are all very happy to be able to make use of a car while at Rimouski.  Readers may recall from a previous chapter that the Yacht Club and nearest grocery store are a considerable distance from each other on-foot.  We arrive back at the boat with a generous amount of food for the crew for their next several days of sailing.  Putting a roast in the oven I ask Chris to check on it and then Don and I go and meet Andrew at the airport as we're on the cusp of another crew turn-over. After waiting what seems like eternity we learn that Andrew's plane is late. We're both relieved when it shows up. Andrew is eager to make his way to the boat, get acquainted with the other crew and get caught up on our progress. It's getting late when we head back to the marina for supper. I'm looking forward to a nice roast beef dinner. I set foot back on the boat and ask how the cooking went, thinking Chris and Jim have taken the roast out of the oven a long, long time ago. Wrong! Opening the oven and lifting the cover I find this wizened-looking remnant of what was supposed to be dinner. The roast comes out of the pan looking small, pathetic and very, very dry. Who needs red meat, anyway? It takes every effort for me not to roll on the floor laughing. The crew end up eating a lot of potatoes tonight.

It doesn't look like much and that's the point. This roast was a lot bigger when it first went into the oven...

Good thing there is a healthy supply of potatoes on the boat at all times!

## Afterward

Bagatelle, Skipper and crew head for the east coast after I depart. Enroute to Gaspé, the boat and crew are caught in a gale-force wind: one of the crew hit the distress button on Don's VHF radio. Two Canadian warships come on-station to aid the boat in seeking safe passage through the tremendous waves. When the ships arrive, Don wonders what assistance they might have in mind; many of their crew are seasick while others manage to take a few photos amidst the chaos. Bagatelle's blue bottom rises above the water-line and then she dissapears save for her mast, storm jib and main. A small figure can be seen at the wheel. During the ensuing chaos, Don is slammed across the pulpit a number of times.

Arriving at a small town in New Brunswick where they can drop anchor, the wind and waves are still fierce. After what seems to be an interminable wait the boat and crew rendezvous with another vessel while at anchor. Don's crew all depart on the aiding boat, leaving him alone to brave the elements. To make matters worse, Bagatelle is disabled! During the chaos her anchor line has come free from storage up by the pulpit and is now wrapped around the boat's prop shaft.

Almost all of Bagatelle's electrical systems are knocked out; in addition, Don loses his glasses during the fray. The boat isn't going anywhere in her present state. On his own, with reduced vision and with no end of foul weather in sight he braves the icy cold of the water to free the boat's prop, with no luck. More time passes before he's assisted by another boat accopmanied by a diver. The diver proceeds to cut away the fouled line, much to Don's chargrin as he would have rather attempted to keep it intact for the remainder of his return trip to Kingston. The incoming crew are alerted to Don's predicament. Instead of meeting him at their original rendezvous, they divert to New Brunswick and find a way to ferry themselves over to the Skipper and his stricken boat.

With new crew finally aboard, Bagatelle is able to resume the return leg of her trip. The boat, Skipper and crew make Gaspé a few days later. Don arrives on shore, locates a land-line and is able to call home. His wife Sylvia already knows about all the trouble he's encountered as both the storm and Bagatelle are featured in the national news.[4] Everyone back home is glad both Don and boat make it back in more-or-less one piece.

| Depart | Arrive | Accum Time on Boat [days] | Accum Time Underway [hours] | Accum Engine Time [hours] | Accum Distance [NM] | Average Speed [kt] |
|---|---|---|---|---|---|---|
| Québec | Cap-à-l'Aigle | 1 | 14.6 | 14.0 | 75.6 | 5.2 |
| Cap-à-l'Aigle | Tadoussac | 1 | 20.7 | 20.2 | 112.9 | 6.1 |
| Tadoussac | Rimouski | 2 | 33.6 | 22.4 | 168.5 | 4.3 |

Engine Time vs Time Underway  66.6%

Time Underway vs Time on Boat  60.1%

Table 4. Trip summary for Bagatelle's voyage from Québec, QC to Rimouski, QC in 2007.

[4] "Ontario-based sloop under escort in rough seas between Quebec and PEI," The Canadian Press, 8 August 2007 11:19 AM

# Chapter 5

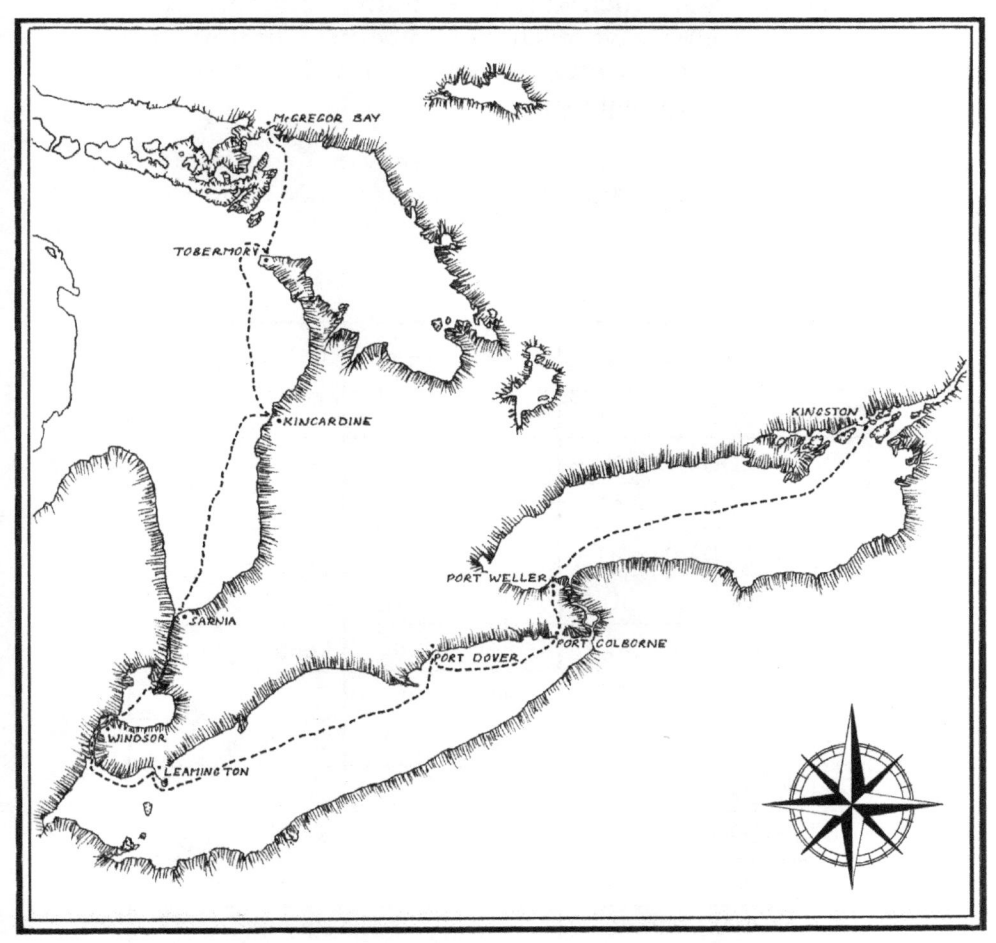

*Kingston, ON to McGregor Bay, ON*

01 to 11 July 2008

The day begins sunny and bright at Kingston Yacht Club, Don is in a bit of a hurry to leave as we're already one day behind from when he'd planned on starting this trip. Our second crewman is already at Bagatelle when I arrive; he informs us one of his friends expects to join us once we reach Port Colborne. Our first stop will be Sugar Loaf Marina with an approximate arrival of 02 July and one anticipated overnight stay.

We consult Don's 2002 log for the previous trip made from Kingston to McGregor Bay. Log entries from 2002 appear in the following Table:

| Date, Time | Depart | Arrive |
|---|---|---|
| 28 June 2002, 15h30 | Kingston | |
| 30 June 2002, 04h10 | | Port Weller |
| 30 June 2002, 04h10 | Port Weller | |
| 30 June 2002, 13h30 | | Port Colborne |
| 01 July 2002, 08h30 | Port Colborne | |
| 03 July 2002, 15h30 | | Leamington |
| 04 July 2002, 08h36 | Leamington | |
| 04 July 2002, 22h00 | | Windsor |
| 05 July 2002, 08h25 | Windsor | |
| 06 July 2002, 01h00 | | Sarnia |
| 06 July 2002, 10h45 | Sarnia | |
| 07 July 2002, 08h45 | | Port Elgin |
| 07 July 2002, 12h30 | Port Elgin | |
| 08 July 2002, 17h10 | | McGregor Bay |

Table 5a: summary of log entries for Bagatelle's 2002 trip from Kingston to McGregor Bay, ON.

Everyone is now aboard and the boat is fuelled and watered. We prepare to cast off while at the same time running a mental list of the stops along Bagatelle's 2002 trip. All of them are decent in terms of crew rest, one might say this will be a "relaxing" trip. Lulled into a false sense of assurance I'm unaware of what the next few days will bring.

## 01 July 2008, Kingston to Port Weller

10h35: slip KYC. Weather: awesome, but little wind.

14h15: south of Pigeon Island, SoG 6 kt, CoG 281°M.

16h06: putting in first reef and change to working jib.

17h02: abeam Psyche Shoal. We eat home-baked lasagna for supper, awesome!

There's a slight haze from the humidity but we're treated to at least four fireworks shows as the sun sets. This is July 1st, Canada Day and a number of towns in and around Prince Edward County on Lake Ontario are putting on impressive shows, all visible from the water.

## 02 July 2008, Enroute to Port Weller

01h26: working jib and one reef in, choppy water.

01h13: it seems to take a long time to pass Port Petre.

04h10: down jib due to lack of wind and lumpy water!

04h45: under sail again, without power.

07h10: change to #2 genny, sunny.

I start feeling worse and heave over the side a few times. I'm given two Gravol to chew. I manage to get one hour of rest in this rough patch of Lake Ontario. We have soup for lunch; I'm at the wheel and fall asleep spilling soup all over myself. All flies out in this part of the lake bite and are quite large in number! It is only a few days into our trip and I realize lake sailing is much different from my previous stints out east. Swells on the Great Lakes have a mind of their own and the wind has a hard time making up its mind. In the absence of wind to keep us on a steady tack, most if not all wave action is uncomfortable for unseasoned crew. With a total lack of wind we're not getting anywhere closer to Welland Canal; Don doesn't appear to be concerned.

12h05: under power due to lack of wind.

19h00: still feeling crappy; I manage to keep down a piece of bread and pistachios. Puking up lasagna isn't fun!

23h00: down sails, under power on approach to canal.

There are tremendous gusts of wind overpower Bagatelle's 21 HP engine as we fight through the waves. The rain is beating sideways and there are a number of shore lights to contend with as crew become frustrated in our search for the entrance to Welland Canal. After what seems like eternity we make the correct lights and alter course. Jutting out from the southern shore of Lake Ontario like a primordial proboscis, the canal's entrance is at least somewhat sheltered as we head towards the first set of locks. I'm thinking of all the places on the great lakes and the St Lawrence waterway, this place could sure benefit from having a set of range lights to establish an appropriate bearing for approaching vessels! Range lights are a navigation aid for vessels to adopt a straight-line course in narrow channels or congested water-ways.

## 03 July 2008, Port Weller to Port Colborne

We arrive at lock #1 at 03h00 and are told we'll have to wait until at least 04h30 before proceeding. Looking for a place to dock, we see a big sign saying "pleasure boats" then "go farther upstream" in much smaller writing underneath. Don is rather leery as he had a near-miss on a previous trip with submerged items in an area close to where the boats are supposed to dock. Bagatelle makes her mooring and I get the best hour of rest I've had in my entire life.

05h45: raining steady, out of lock #1.

06h35: out of lock #2.

Coming up to the first set of locks in the Welland Canal at dawn.

07h13: out of lock #3.

08h04: out of lock #4.

08h36: out of lock #5. The size of each set of locks is beyond belief! Proceeding from one to the next we seem to encounter doors bigger than the last. The volume of water required to fill each lock must be down-right ridiculous!

08h59: out of lock #6. We have to wait for lock #7 as they have a hydraulic leak. We eat an excellent breakfast while we wait.

11h17: out of lock #7.

14h14: out of lock #8.

14h24: out of the canal and into Lake Erie.

The walls of each lock tower above us as we wait for the next set of doors to open.

15h24: arrive at Sugar Loaf Marina, F24, 68Mhz.

## 04 July 2008, Port Colborne to Port Dover

Don and I awake to find the other crewman has disappeared during the night. A few of his belongings remain; it's almost as if he departed in a hurry. We are aware it might be on account of a family matter but can't be sure. His wife neither confirms nor denies she's heard from him. Both Don and I are upset since he leaves without advance notice or payment of his share of the fuel, food and $200.00 lock fee for going through the Welland Canal. To make matters worse the fourth crewman, whom we thought would be joining us at Port Colborne, never shows up. This brings our number down to two people aboard Bagatelle for the foreseeable future. It is frustrating as we won't do well with so few people on the boat and with much of the voyage still ahead of us!

10h30: take on 30.4L of diesel, $50.40 for fuel and $15.00 for sewage pump-out.

Sugar Loaf is an excellent(!) marina. They appear to host a good number of well-off patrons so it's a matter of not needing money from tourists and transients to survive. Internet/WiFi and showers are complimentary. We end up having to pay for our sewage pump-out as we are at the fuel dock when it happens. Don finds out later that the marina could have done it for free.

11h00: Don and Eric leave Port Colborne.

15h06: under power since leaving the marina, flat seas and no clouds, beautiful weather! SoG 6.4 kt, CoG 254°M.

15h30: smoke in the cockpit. I try to tell Don it is coming out of the cabinets where the fenders are kept but he doesn't believe me. I pull the engine cover off to find smoke billowing from the engine.

16h00: return line to #3 fuel injector re-connected after much searching for small hose clamps.

16h30: engine still spurting fuel, I take the air filter off to get a better look. Fuel sprays everywhere when Don cycles power. All neighboring food and boat's contents are now soaked in diesel.

A tremendous quantity of fuel issues forth like a manic geyser with each turn of the ignition in our attempts to locate the leak. By now, I'm reasoning the heat from Bagatelle's engine is causing this excessive spray of diesel to cook off from various parts such as the exhaust manifold. After many, many seasons of sailing, engine trouble aboard the boat is something unusual as the performance from Don's 21Hp Japanese diesel is rock-steady. On her worst days at sea, the boat is jostled in all directions: hours upon hours her screw is subjected to a frenetic punishment of free wheeling in thin air to then being forced back into the water with all ten tons of boat working against it. Therefore, this latest trouble must not be anything too serious and so I continue to troubleshoot the spiderweb of fuel lines.

1730: fuel pump cycled. I determine the leak is coming from a kinked fuel line.

19h30: the damaged fuel line is replaced with tubing from Don's fuel transfer kit; a temporary fix. Engine is bled and started. Under power for Port Dover it is going to be tight depth-wise. Expected time-of-arrival (ETA) is 11h00.

21h05: We speak with Port Dover marina, our slip will be 13A. They instruct us to stay close to the breakwater as depth gets close to 6.9 ft in places.

23h00: Don is nervous about coming in with little to no visibility. Two cans (buoys) appear on radar once we are almost on top of them. The depth comes to less than 1.7m in places once we are in the marina.

23h15: moor at Port Dover Marina.

24h00: we sit down to eat the chicken souvlaki left behind by the departed crewman. Why the Hell did he leave? Alien abduction?

## 05 July 2008, Port Dover to Leamington

12h00: get fuel, 22.8L at $29.26. Docking fee is $60.00. After much walking, we manage to get a proper 3/8-inch fuel line from a marine supply store. Not at all convenient to get to for boaters! We make good on our departure with half of the day behind us. Our delay is not bad when we learn marine rates are $85.00/hr.

12h40: depart Port Dover, Don scrapes bottom once.

13h00: further trouble with fuel lines, I work on them and hope they will not leak again. Problem is with dissimilar pipe diameters at each end. We have to sail for a while as work is in progress on the engine.

All of our hopes in getting back on course and making good progress towards McGregor Bay are dashed when the engine begins to die. By now I'm somewhat of an expert at ripping the crew ladder away and throwing the hatch open. Once again our attempts to repair the engine have failed as the intake hose has come loose, spurting fuel everywhere. Its hose clamp is re-tightened and this time the fix seems to work.

13h30: we resume course to take us around Long Point. Under power as we have lost a lot of time.

With the unscheduled stop at Port Dover, we've added a rather large amount of distance to this trip. Long Point juts out into Lake Erie and is preventing us from taking a direct passage to Leamington. Had we sailed from Port Colborne, without stopping in Port Dover and notwithstanding winds we could have kept Long Point to starboard all across Lake Erie.

16h30: smoke is still coming from the engine hatch, we may need to re-tighten the fuel injector lines or other return lines. The intake line seems to be doing fine.

16h35: round Long Point.

18h40: the roast goes in Bagatelle's oven at 350°F.

19h30: the third time this hour the Coast Guard has had to warn other boats to get the Hell off channel 16.

As mentioned in a previous chapter, Channel 16 is reserved for emergencies. Most marine traffic, Coast Guard and shore-based shipping services stay on this channel until two or more parties need to communicate amongst each other. One of the parties announces to the others which channel to switch to, ideally one that isn't being used by other traffic so they can resume discussions without tying up other traffic.

20h30: under power again, all return lines and clamps replaced, leak check, everything seems okay.

21h10: roast out. Definitely better than the one from our 2007 trip!

23h50: sea at dead calm.

This voyage, like all the others I've taken aboard Bagatelle is a chance to get to know Canada. I've come to appreciate taking trips by boat can be rewarding as one gains a true dependence on the people and places at each port-of-call. The elements are much more raw and open when you are alone on the water with a few shreds of fabric to keep the warmth in. Tonight the stars are out in full force, unobstructed by city lights or smog.

A couple of days ago I didn't know much about the Great Lakes or what people are like here. Fishing seems to happen but not a lot of commercial operations remain. Our stop in Port Dover, although unexpected is quite pleasant with houses and buildings nestled into the hills alongside Lake Erie.

## 06 July 2008, Enroute to Leamington

00h55: hoist #2 genny. Wind has come up at 6.6 kt, 55° off starboard bow. Small gain in speed. May shut off engine if wind increases.

01h05: wind rising out of west-north-west at 7.5 to 8.0 kt.

01h10: increased list to port, engine off and going under sails.

01h18: SoG 5.6 kt, CoG 260°M. Awesome!

03h00: lots of stars out tonight.

Motoring towards Windsor with a freighter coming up on our stern.

Alone in the cockpit, I'm aware of the dangerous lack of crew on our trip. My first time aboard Bagatelle, at night, with less than two people awake for any reasonable amount of time. Extra care needs to be taken with each movement when relieving oneself off the stern. Any sudden motion from the waves could knock a person over the edge, with a faint hope one's harness will remain intact. With the autohelm engaged and engine running I'll have no hope of signalling Don I've fallen overboard. Lake Erie is large enough to force me to believe rescue would not happen for days, if at all.

03h42: down jib, run engine as wind dies off.

06h18: have to alter course to south in order to point boat towards buoys off Pelee Island.

08h00: assuming constant speed, ETA at Pelee Point is 15h45.

08h26: fighting fierce battle with flies.

09h45: calm, no wind, lots of flies. Spare battery for Don's cell phone does not fit his phone. After one call it is down to three bars and we are too far from land for it to be used.

15h50: alongside buoy E8 by Pelee Passage.

16h00: speaking with Leamington Marina, they inform us they have 9 ft of uniform depth, no reservations . They are open until 22h00, the fuel dock closes at 21h00. Docking will be port-side, call on channel 68 once we reach the entrance.

17h45: arrive Leamington Marina, re-fuel, 55.2L at $76.73. Docking fees are $60.00.

Once we are moored Don tries to call David, a friend located in Kincardine. We're hoping he'll want to join us for at least part of this trip.

## 07 July 2008, Leamington to Windsor

The Skipper makes his way into town in search of replacement parts for his cell phone. In addition to a weak battery, Don's phone isn't getting a lot of coverage on the lakes. My cell works fine, both in view of land and on wide-open water. After much walking Don is disappointed to learn they don't carry any batteries at the retail outlet. This store seems to be more in the business of selling new phones. The coverage map they provide isn't much comfort either since most of the area over open water has proven difficult, despite claims to the contrary by their marketing department. Bottom line, though, is we have my cell plus VHF so line-of-sight communication isn't an issue for this trip.

11h20: slip Leamington marina. Sunny, hot, humid with #2 genny and main up.

12h53: David responds to Don's voicemail, he would like more details about our trip. We're hopeful he'll be able to join us.

13h00: under power and sail.

15h33: flies are terrible! Torture!

We reach Don's friend David and provide him with an update on our progress. Don and I apprise him of the situation we're in with the lack of crew. This will be the last time we hear from him on this trip.

16h25: Canadian Progress passes us going up-bound.

16h30: American Courage passes down-bound with somewhat dirty exhaust.

The freighters in this part of the St Lawrence seaway are known as "lakers." They are different from other vessels we've encountered farther east of Kingston. The bridges on lakers are painted in bright white and most are situated above the forecastle, as far forward as possible. The bows on these vessels are also rather blunt.

16h50: autopilot is erratic.

A number of electrical systems aboard Bagatelle give us trouble on this trip. I recount a number of items Don has had me repair over the past few years but this trip it seems like the number is growing. A few items are quick to fix including an errant connection to one of the circuit breakers in addition to the boat's horn that has a loose wire under one of the lockers in the cockpit. Despite these successes there isn't much I can do for the autopilot which works on an intermittent basis. Without access to the right test equipment I cannot do much to determine the cause of the problem. Dismay sets in as both Don and I know full well the extent of work needed to keep the boat on course in rough weather in absence of the autopilot. Although we've encountered little to no wind across Lake Erie, we know there is a lot of water yet to cover.

16h58: passing Bois Blanc Island.

17h39: take down the main as a rain squall hits us. Current is 1.7 kt, speed-over-water 5.4 kt. We pass Amberstburg.

19h00: passing Grosse Island.

19h20: close to buoy 94, passing Grassy Island.

20h05: we pass Milo (Neipaiaz) on our starboard side.

21h50: dock at Morton Terminal off the Detroit River. Looks like a nice place to spend the night.

Detroit and Windsor, while similar in certain respects, are cities in contrast. At the time of our trip there is still a hum and buzz of activity in so many steel mills and various plants across the border while Canadian companies appear to be focused on exports, with many terminals off-loading raw goods onto freighters. We are encouraged when we see at least one company in full production of wind turbine equipment: massive propellers and sections of tower are lined up along the water's edge, ready to be shipped.

22h00: a security guard approaches Bagatelle as we finish dinner. We manage to convince him we still have engine trouble and intend to leave at crack of dawn.

Heat and humidity are intense as we head north. Detroit is to port, Windsor to starboard.

Our stop at Morton Terminal comes late in the evening and we're in no mood to continue searching for better locations. The dock walls are high and covered in large tires to act as fenders for tankers. Don and I have to do a bit of climbing to make it to the top and secure docking lines. When a security guard comes to check on us he is very polite but indicates we'll have to find somewhere else to spend the night. Well, shit. Thinking fast and having had trouble with engine I have no difficulty telling him we've stopped for the night on account of safety. He heads off for a quick smoke, then returns and makes us promise we won't leave the boat while we're docked. We promise him we'll be heading off early the next morning.

Another late meal and then it's off to bed. Up in the forward berth I'm uncomfortable as there is no air flow in this dead calm, tremendous heat and humidity. I'm sweating in my sleep throughout the rest of the night.

## 08 July 2008, Windsor to Sarnia

06h50: slipped in a grey morning, windy and very humid!

07h35: under Ambassador Bridge.

08h00: arrive at Lake St Claire.

Wind, glorious wind! A steady breeze is growing stronger each minute as we make our way out into the open water, eager to hoist sails. Don convinces me everything is under control topside so I head below to make breakfast. After the business we've encountered these past few days I reckon it's time we get something decent to eat. Scrambled eggs with onions, cheese and seasoning complimented with potatoes, green pepper and onion topped off with toast and coffee. We're topside finishing the last few bites when a search-and-rescue helicopter zooms by. The crew of the helicopter appears to be out on exercise today as they approach another vessel and enter hover for quite a while.

09h15: pass Pêche Island.

09h40: abeam second range light in Fleming Channel.

16h05: 28°C in the shade, no wind, humidex at 100%?

Something remarkable is happening as we approach Sarnia. The color of the water is getting bluer and bluer the farther north we travel! It is in vivid contrast to the deep-grey hues on the Atlantic and tinges of green in other parts of the St Lawrence Seaway.

17h10: pass Canadian Enterprise offloading coal at power station.

20h15: under Blue Water Bridge in Sarnia.

We're in view of the Yacht Club at Sarnia, I'm ready with fenders and boat hooks but Don is hesitant to enter as we're now past the bridge and a strong north-east wind is making navigation difficult. Top it off with a strong current with the mouth of the river adjacent to the club entrance in addition to little margin of error on depth and we're being careful on ingress. Don makes a few attempts before settling on a preferred course into the club.

He recalls the last time at Sarnia when he had to be hauled off the rocks by the Junior Sailing Squadron. We make our way into the entrance and secure mooring.

21h00: arrive at Sarnia Yacht Club. I'm struck by how clear the water is around here! We meet Lindy as well as Steve who owns a 1971 C&C 35. They welcome us to the yacht club. We end up with a complimentary stay despite having access to showers/water/shore power. This is quite in contrast to Don's trip in 2002 where they had to pay $2.20/ft at Sarnia Marina. Fuel tank topped up with 43.63L, $45.28! Awesome!

Supper doesn't turn out quite like I'd hoped: we've got a tremendous amount of ground beef on-board that needs to be used up before it spoils so tonight it's meat with a side of more meat. All complaining aside, left-overs are a Godsend in the coming days.

## 09 July 2008, Sarnia to Kincardine

08h45: slip fuel dock, don't have to pay $40.00 overnight docking fee. Weather sunny and clear, wind 10-15 kt.

09h17: a wind warning is issued for northern part of Lake Huron. Southern portion showing wind from south-west at 10 kt, changing to north-west later today. No call for showers or thunderstorms.

10h16: under sail with main and working jib, SoG 6.1 kt, CoG 31°M.

10h25: we're hit with a sudden squall, ruining once-perfect course!

11h00: loss of suction on the head.

12h27: change from #2 genny to working jib, wind gauge shows 10.8 kt and more.

The wind can't make up its mind on this leg of our trip! Changing sails aboard Bagatelle is a job for at least two people under normal circumstances. One person mans the winch for the halyard and a second person stays close to the clew of the sail, reaching up to grab portions of sail as it is lowered. The second crewman works their way forward as the sail comes down. In the case of the jib the person will use their whole body to keep the sail from flapping away in the wind. Flaking the sail and lashing it once it is down is also much easier if there are two people.

Don and I determine it will be easier for us to leave the non-flying jib lashed forward. Given the sudden changes in wind coupled with rough water, this strategy ends up paying dividends. We're soon at a point where one person is able to change sails, albeit slower than when we had the luxury of more crew. Frustration sets in when raising and lowering the main in this confused wind as the halyard gets wrapped around the shrouds a number of times. Intransigence of Bagatelle's bits and pieces is something we can do without on this trip!

13h15: take down working jib as wind has died, engine started.

16h06: 43°26.9'N, 82°07.7'W, SoG 6.3 kt, CoG 31°M. Running with engine and #2 genny to help keep boat stable.

18h17: flies are terrible! Many many many!

19h17: engine off, under sail.

19h45: #2 genny down, wind coming right in the direction we need to go, gusting up to 14 kt. I fabricate a couple of additional sail-ties from a length of "non-sacred" rope.

Every piece of halyard, sheet and line aboard Bagatelle has a specific purpose and while plentiful each one is reserved and thus protected from would-be do-it-yourselfers looking for a short section for one miscellaneous reason or another. I manage to convince Don to part with older, smaller rope that will certainly be useful as a makeshift sail-tie.

20h07: sudden shift in wind with big increase in velocity.

20h39: second reef in main.

## 10 July 2008, Enroute to Kincardine

The wind is intense on our approach and Don is aware of an unmarked, unlit breakwater from previous trips. We consult some of the charts and pubs aboard for this area to confirm the location of the breakwater. Bagatelle's progress towards our mooring for tonight is, of course, slow as we jostle our way through the lumpy water and wrestle in near total darkness with securing sails. Passing the breakwater, the waves calm a bit as we arrive at one of the docks.

02h58: secure at Kincardine Yacht Club.

We wake up at 08h00 and get fuel, 30.3L at $47.05. Going up a hill from the Marina in search of groceries, I marvel at yet another small town along the Great Lakes having pride in its appearance. The weather here is different than what we've experienced earlier on this trip: dry and sunny but less humid and cooler than Sarnia and in stark contrast to Windsor though we're not much farther north. One quick stop at their hardware store is needed to secure fly paper. We're under constant barrage by flies leaving nasty bite marks. They seem to linger on the boat regardless of how far out in the water we go, or how strong the wind is. Back aboard Bagatelle I set to work stringing traps at various points, taking care not to come into contact.

### 10 July 2008, Kincardine to Tobermory

10h45: slipped, sunny and warm.

12h33: very lumpy water with little wind on the nose.

Don comes into contact with one of the fly traps as he makes his way forward in the cabin, there is inaudible cussing as this happens. I convince him it's a small price to pay to get the bug situation under control. We find out we have a day or so to wait for the traps to have their intended effect. I get caught myself and find out it isn't fun. These traps work well but they sure do leave an awful mess on a person's clothes!

12h58: little to no wind.

There is very little shipping traffic in this part of Lake Huron and discernable lack of small pleasure boats. Very quiet compared to our passage through Lake Erie. With no wind I have this feeling of sensory deprivation as we make our way north-west.

13h40: we pick up a large metallic balloon from the water. A few days before, Eric recovered a Doritos bag. Judging from the condition of both of these items and being they are out in open water, this trash must have come from other boats. The water here is so clear, it is upsetting that people hurl their garbage over the side!

15h20: despite lumpy sea Don has a good sleep. Still unable to sail as there is little breeze but lots of swell.

We get two MAFOR updates in the afternoon, each one calls for little to no wind with a small chance of rain. The wave action, thudding of the engine and lack of sleep are putting me in a trance-like state. Don asks me to troubleshoot his older GPS as the chart program on the computer is no longer getting our current position. We have a new plotter on this trip with its own GPS; however, it tends to lose position as the antenna is located inside the cabin.

Radio traffic is lighter out in this part of Lake Huron in contrast to our voyage across Lake Erie. On any given day there are three or more distress calls. Most are false, with the Coast Guard having to continue to query the vessel or aircraft to confirm if they are in trouble or not. One boat is reported on fire, another overturned, other problems hard to make out. All of the traffic comes from Coast Guard stations; we extrapolate what the trouble is by the questions they ask.

20h49: 45°03.9'N, 81°46.5'W, SoG 2.9 kt, CoG 10°M. Heavy north-east wind, weather people are out to lunch!

Supper is left-over ground beef, again, but no complaints as we are in rough water with a lot of attention focused on getting Bagatelle to her next stop. An ominous black cloud forms at nightfall, obliterating any hope of ambient light. Concern develops over the sudden excessive wind and I'm fearful we'll be in a down-pour at any second. Reviewing the charts for our approach through Devils Island Channel, I do a double-take when realizing that the three buoys marking the sides of the challen are all in-line with each other. Having no other option to transition between Lake Huron and Georgian Bay, we press onward.

22h35: new course once at FIG (flashing green) buoy by Devil's Island Channel is 40° true. Don is steering by compass on starboard side. Heading for Tobermory as winds expected to prevent us from making significant progress tonight.

It is after eleven when we encounter the first buoy in the channel. Both GPS are acting erratic and reporting incomprehensible courses and speeds. Without warning they quit working on us! The compasses aboard Bagatelle each report different headings and at one point I swear I see one of them spinning wildly as we make our way through the channel. The winds have subsided, thank God, but this jubilation is overshadowed when we encounter a 5-6 knot current sucking and pulling everything towards multiple rocky outcrops hidden beneath the water's surface. There is no break in the clouds so we are shrouded in total darkness. With both GPS off-line and questionable compasses all we're left with is the radar to keep us lined up with each buoy. Bagatelle is making progress towards the second can so I make my way topside to light it up and help Don avoid hitting it. The big yellow spotlight flickers then dies! A few knocks and still no luck; it is about to get ejected over the side of the boat when it sputters back to life. Now we're on top of the can and I'm screaming at Don "hard to starboard!" The boat comes close enough for us to almost smell the seagull guano on top of the buoy! Corrections are made just in time and in a few more minutes we're away from this treacherous channel and getting into deeper and deeper water. Both GPS are still off-line, so I glue myself to the radar and call out distances and estimated bearings to keep Don off Devil's Island Bank. The radar provides a decent return from various points of land with which to navigate and so we continue without further incident to Tobermory.

## 11 July 2008, at Tobermory

00h03: tie up at Tobermory fuel dock.

It's so bloody cold here! Getting ready for bed, I discover my sleeping bag is soaked from leaving the forward hatch open. I get little to no sleep on account of having a towel for a blanket. Awesome.

Don is as tough as nails. The reason we stop in Tobermory is because he thinks I might get sick in the pitching and stormy sea during the night. By this time in our trip I pretty much have my sea legs but don't mind the stop at all. Between the extreme heat and humidity of Windsor, flies and mosquitoes at Kincardine and biting cold at Tobermory I get little to no sleep most nights. The Skipper is up at the crack of dawn each day!

## 11 July 2008, Tobermory to McGregor Bay

An attendant helps us get water and fuel, 28.9L for $45.35. She has a feathered friend named "Jonathan Seagull" who's followed her around the dock for the past few years. For food I imagine.

07h45: slipped.

08h45: beside Echo Island.

09h30: GPS and autohelm both go offline without tripping circuit breakers... Weird. We spin around and head back to Tobermory!

Don tries to contact the people who provide MAFORs over VHF. We want to find out when each of the forecasts are supposed to start. They don't give us a clear answer, suggesting they don't know either. Not a lot of trust in their forecasts after yesterdays' events!

At this point in the trip we do not need to rely on GPS as Don is in familiar water and the day is bright and sunny. We make a few more attempts to trouble-shoot enroute to McGregor Bay with mixed success.

Brisk sailing enroute to McGregor Bay.

11h40: passing Club Island (north side). Wind is passing from east to north-east, making jib unworkable. Proceed with main and engine.

13h59: sunny, warm and little wind. Swells have diminished. Another fine lunch by Eric.

14h15: abeam of Cape Smith.

18h30: drop anchor at McGregor Bay. There is one spot in the entire bay suitable for Bagatelle to weigh anchor and Don knows it well.

Don and his father built their cottage in 1941. Several families lived close to each other on various islands; this is where Don and Sylvia met. President Roosevelt came up here in the 1940s for a fishing trip prior to the Québec Summit. The whole set of islands is majestic yet rugged, speaking to the tenacity of the people who build cottages here. Don and Sylvia's cottage on Eagle Island is nice, albeit rustic. McGregor bay is rocky with little beach area. The water is quite cold. Hydrographic datum suggest water level is up over the past few years.

One of many rugged and majestic islands in McGregor Bay.

## Afterward

If Don writes any thankyou letters the first should go to the company who manufactures his radar. A second letter should go to the Japanese company responsible for designing and building Bagatelle's engine. The fuel leak is a minor annoyance compared to much more serious trouble such as losing the engine from rocking in and out of the water in heavy swells.

Like all other trips, the Skipper ensures the boat is well-prepared with numerous charts and books. A couple of his charts date back to 1940 and are surveyed as far back as 1876. Despite their age, they are of immense benefit due to an incredible amount of soundings, topography and land-mass detail you don't find on modern charts. Soundings are spaced close together in shallow areas. As for age, Don offers obvious reassurance that despite the passing decades, "rocks don't move much." In addition to charts we end up consulting numerous books to determine depth, point of entry, services and navigation aids for places such as Tobermory, Sarnia and Kincardine. It is useful to have this information aboard, as we found out on our approach to Kincardine with the unlit, unmarked breakwater!

This is the most challenging trip I've ever taken aboard the boat on account of lack of crew, set-backs with the engine and electrical systems, extremes in temperature not to mention thousands of flies that take huge chomps out of people. Most of the time I felt like we were running rum and spices back to the old country! In 2002, Don and a full complement of crew made it in eleven days. This trip in 2008 sees us with a one-day delay at the start. We are further delayed by over a day when the engine trouble starts. We also have to backtrack to resume our course across Lake Erie once we depart Port Dover in order to clear Long Point. Everything seems compounded by the sheer lack of people to crew, cook and clean in addition to all of the other matters one encounters while sailing. We make the trip in ten days, regardless of all of the delays and side-trips.

| Depart | Arrive | Accum Time on Boat [days] | Accum Time Underway [hours] | Accum Engine Time [hours] | Accum Distance [NM] | Average Speed [kt] |
|---|---|---|---|---|---|---|
| Kingston | Port Weller | 2 | 40.4 | Not available | 143.1 | 3.5 |
| Port Weller | Port Colborne | 2 | 50.1 | 14.3 | 165.3 | 2.3 |
| Port Colborne | Port Dover | 4 | 62.3 | 23.5 | 211.9 | 3.8 |
| Port Dover | Leamington | 5 | 91.4 | 46.9 | 364.7 | 5.3 |
| Leamington | Windsor | 6 | 101.9 | 54.8 | 406.6 | 4.0 |
| Windsor | Sarnia | 7 | 116.1 | 68.8 | 467.1 | 4.3 |
| Sarnia | Kincardine | 9 | 134.3 | 84.0 | 551.8 | 4.7 |
| Kincardine | Tobermory | 10 | 147.6 | 98.0 | 633.4 | 6.1 |
| Tobermory | McGregor Bay | 10 | 158.3 | 108.8 | 697.1 | 5.9 |

Engine Time vs Time Underway  68.7%

Time Underway vs Time on Boat  63.9%

Table 5b. Trip summary for Bagatelle's voyage from Kingston, ON to McGregor Bay, ON in 2008.

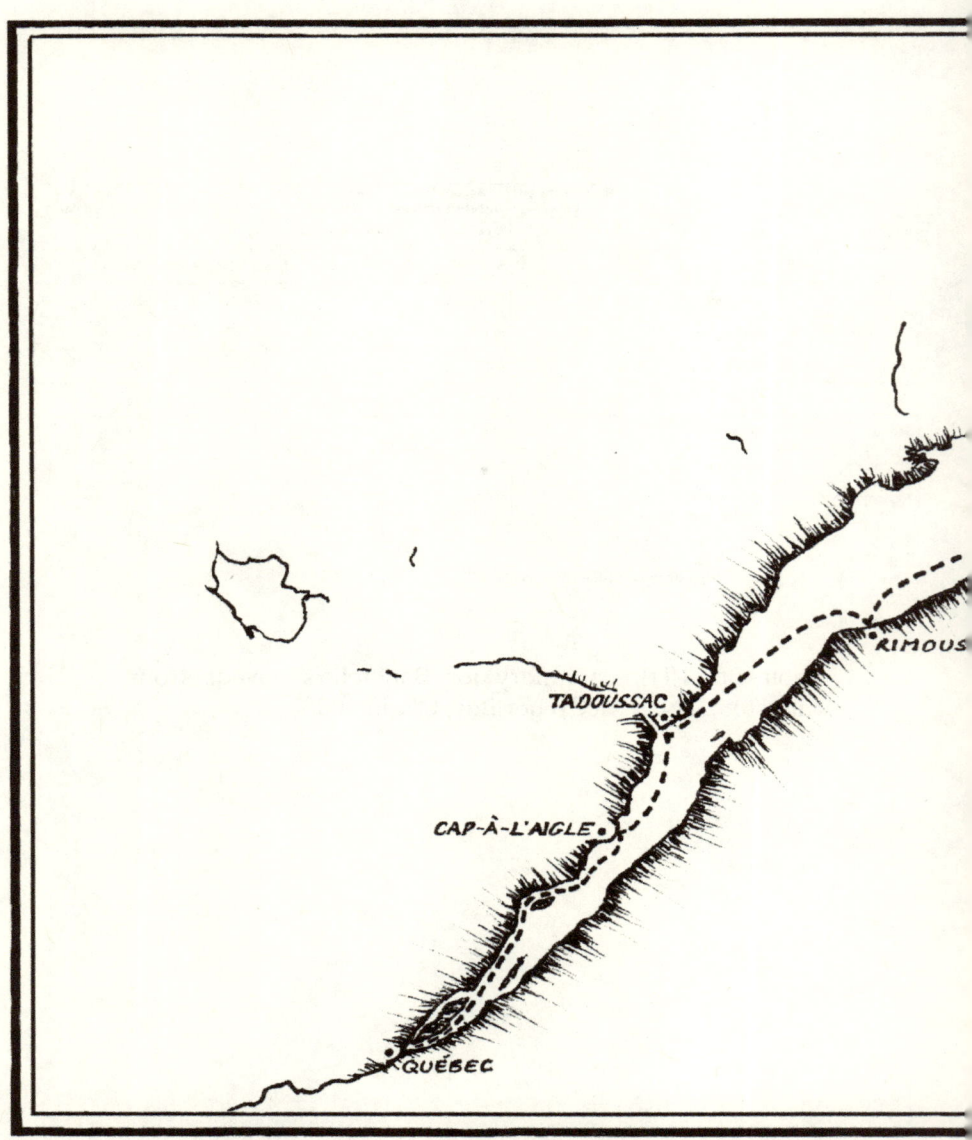

# Chapter 6

*Gaspé, QC to Québec, QC*

**29 July to 04 August 2010**

Two years have passed since my last major excursion aboard Bagatelle and I'm looking forward to what I hope will be good sailing. I make my way eastward from Belleville by train, with a transfer in Montréal. The train ride from Montréal to Gaspé aboard VIA Rail is elegant and retro. Nice dinner in their dining car; no reservations mean you sit with whomever else hasn't made any. Decent prices and food is good, considering we're held hostage out in the middle of nowhere. All of the staff aboard the train are very accommodating. If you ever have occasion to make this trip I recommend taking a sleeper coach. The extra expense is well-worth the leg room, comfort and amenities!

## 29 July 2010, At Gaspé

My train arrives in Gaspé one hour late; Don greets me at the platform. The marina is a few feet from the train station! On the way to the boat Don provides me with updates on Bagatelle's condition. I'm informed that the ice-box is broken. Don settled for a repair that doesn't work, despite the availability of a spare compressor and other parts during Bagatelle's stop in Halifax earlier this trip. The holding tank has diesel in it; Don tells me he's made a tremendous effort in attempting to purge it. I've brought a small, hand-powered water filter and resolve to use it for all of our potable water on this trip.

I come aboard the boat and get settled in. Yup, the water does have a funny taste to it. Looks like my water filter is going to see a lot of action on this trip. Alain (our second crewman) arrives later in the afternoon and we prepare to set sail at first light.

## 30 July 2010, Gaspé to Rivière-au-Renard

07h40: Don, Eric and Alain slipped, cloudy but bright out.

09h04: back under sail with two reefs, wind increasing, several knots made good.

10h14: beside Cap Gaspé.

10h38: surprise, the second reef comes in handy, lumpy seas and wind is up to 29 kt at 60° apparent.

Alain at the helm; air is crisp and cool as we make our way to Rivière-au-Renard.

18h34: engine started on account of slow progress through strong wind on the nose.

19h10: SoG 4.2 kt, 5 NM out from Rivière-au-Renard. Will stop for the night since making little progress in this wind.

22h00: secure at Rivière-au-Renard.

Good sailing the entire afternoon although we cover little distance. I'm sick twice as we pitch through the swells. After a couple years of sailing I'm not that concerned as it takes a day or two for me to get my sea-legs. Making Riviere-au-Renard late in the evening, I cook way too much penne. We sit down to supper at 23h00. Alain and I prepare Bagatelle for the night by securing her halyards to one of the shrouds with a small length of line. In the shelter of the harbour the wind somehow reaches in and jostles all of the boats. Loose halyards will be slammed into the mast throughout the night making sleep difficult for the occupants of Bagatelle as well as neighbouring boats.

Alain and I take turns filtering water from Bagatelle's holding tank. It helps remove the smell of fuel oil and chlorine.

## 31 July 2010, at Rivière-au-Renard

After a great sleep, I awake to find +20 knot winds inside the harbour and the air is bitter cold. I dub this month "Juctober." We're not going to continue the trip this morning. Part of the main is tattered and in rough shape, one of the crew attempted to repair it prior to my arrival in Gaspé. I set to work on an improved repair and use several strips of adhesive-backed fabric to distribute wind loads away from the damage. The strips are arranged in a fan-shaped pattern, one over-top of the other. Although the new repair takes me a few hours to complete it pays dividends for us later in the trip when we encounter wind gusts.

We make a short trip into town after breakfast: Don finds batteries for his binoculars. We stop at the Poissonerie for fresh salmon and crab legs, yes man! Walking back to the marina we make a quick stop at their interpretive centre, this town is big on cod fishing. There are decent showers and other facilities close to the marina.

Don's binoculars don't seem to work after battery replacement. The binoculars have an electronic compass integrated into the optics and you are supposed to be able to obtain a reading of your heading, based on the direction the binoculars are pointing. The built-in compass is a desirable feature as navigators are able to call out headings and course corrections for the boat based on landmarks.

Bagatelle moored in the shelter of a generous breakwater at Rivière-au-Renard.

It's the middle of the day, I know it's supposed to be July but it feels like late Fall! What happened to our warm summer weather at Gaspé? The wind cuts to the bone and there's no respite from the cold in this bright and sunny afternoon. We hope that the winds will calm down enough for us to leave the harbour and continue our journey. Don intends for Bagatelle to reach Québec City with at least one day to spare before the next crew change.

15h15: winds diminishing, looks like we're going to make a run for it. Someone tell the weatherman he's out-to-lunch! We make a final trip to the small grocery/convenience store to keep our fish cool until tomorrow night.

17h33: wind dropping from 30 down to 15 kt but a big rolling sea still coming in from the north. One day sailing to Ste Anne-des-Monts, another to Rimouski and still another to Tadoussac.

18h45: making preparations for departure, quarter-berth is somewhat dry. Gentleman from Georgian Bay comes to visit us in the afternoon, he has a cottage close to Don's in McGregor Bay. They're sailing in a steel hull called "Tulak," heading for Nova Scotia to dock for the season.

## 31 July 2010, Rivière-au-Renard to Ste Anne-des-Monts

19h06: leave Rivière-au-Renard, wind decreased.

19h30: pass "Groupe CTMA," ocean liner/ferry.

20h05: abeam Pointe de l'Échouerie.

21h15: finish hot dog supper.

Instead of boiling hot dogs I opt to cook them on the mock toaster on top of Don's stove. It takes a few attempts before cooking is satisfactory as they tend to burn and get stuck to the hot metal. The boat begins to smell like a chip truck.

21h30: Alain off to sleep.

21h35: winds coming up from the south, we will put the main up but keep two reefs in. Coming up on Pointe-à-la-Renommée.

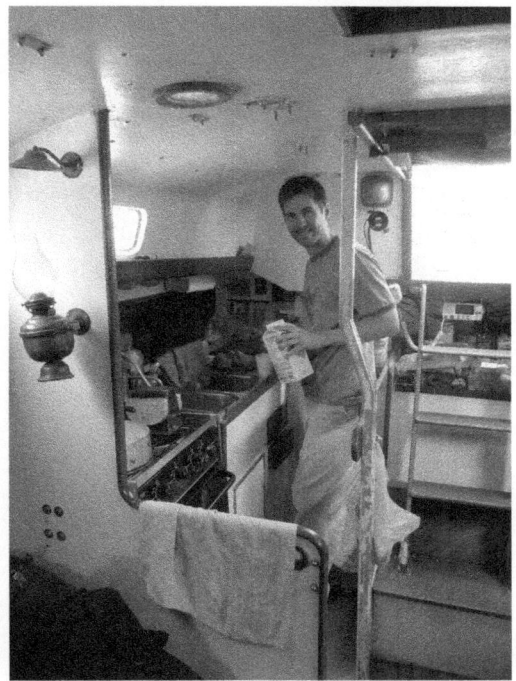

Eric preparing lunch (note toaster on top of stove).

## 01 August 2010, Enroute to Ste Anne-des-Monts

00h11: bright moon!

01h49: close to Grande-Vallée. Winds are up to 28 kt for a short while.

03h00: pass Cap-de-la-Madeleine.

03h30: Eric up, Don goes to sleep. F*** is it cold outside!

04h29: beside St-Antoine-de-Gros-Morne, round Gaspé peninsula.

06h00: abeam freighter, winds pick up from south-west at 20 kt.

Sunrise is a sight to behold with scattered clouds. The cold and unforgiving sea begins to reveal itself as the firmaments separate with the onset of a soft orange glow in the east. Sight of land on our port and an endless expanse of water off starboard become more and more prominent with each passing second. A strong wind carries the coldest part of the Gulf into every fibre of our being; we're indebted to any shelter afforded by the transition of the cockpit to the cabin. Up at the wheel, I'm hunkered down as much as possible and sheathed in so many layers of rain gear, sou'wester, boots, gloves, hood, sweater, anything to keep from getting hypothermia as we press onward.

06h30: Don up, Alain goes for nap, Eric thereafter.

07h00: pass Point des Bernier.

11h40: close to St-Joachim-de-Tourelle.

12h19: secure at Sainte-Anne-des-Monts, add 40L in total to aft and forward tanks.

Amazing sunset as we make our way along the north-east coast of Gaspé.

We have an excellent lunch at the Poissonerie on the other side of their science centre, $25.00 including tip for Table d'hôte. Fish soup, Main Crocques de Mere and lemon meringue pie. Don and Alain come close to having to pry my fingers off the table as I'm quite content to stay here and indulge until I explode.

## 01 August 2010, Ste Anne-des-Monts to Rimouski

15h20: slip Sainte-Anne-des-Monts.

17h30: alongside whales sounding and hill full of wind turbines. No luck this afternoon with either the working jib or tall-boy, both are taken down.

18h51: sunny, no wind. Pass les Méchins. Supper is crab leg and pan-fried salmon. Excellent!

As far as I'm concerned the food on this trip is some the best I've had both on and off the boat. It makes up for all of the hectic and tumultuous progress we're making with a stubborn wind right on our nose. As we continue to alter to port in coming around the bulbous nose of the Gaspé peninsula the wind makes a corresponding shift. Don is determined to set as direct a course as possible to get to Rimouski and so we continue under engine, day and night.

23h11: mystery light off port bow, flashes three times once every 3 to 6 seconds. Radar shows something in front of us at 2 NM, keeping pace.

23h40: mystery light is Pointe-Mitis, FL(3) 7 1/2 seconds 24 metres. Still have contact on radar in front, now 2.5 NM away.

## 02 August 2010, Enroute to Rimouski

00h45: pass ferry closing awful fast on starboard, have to correct to port to avoid her.

03h27: abeam of Pointe-Mitis, light is bright!

04h25: pass Pointe aux Cenelles.

05h24: red fishing vessel off port.

06h16: passing l'Anse-aux-Coques.

07h44: secure at Rimouski. Engine hours: 2530.4, hours since last refuel: 2514.0. At a burn rate of 2L/hr, we expect to take on 32.8L.

We take on 31.7L of diesel, the holding tank for water is replenished as well. Everyone has an awesome crepe breakfast at "Capitainerie" above the marina. I'm drowsy as I eat and am looking forward to making at least one decent overnight stop on this trip. The showers at this marina are expensive, but much-needed!

## 02 August 2010, Rimouski to Tadoussac

10h35: slipped.

14h00: pass south-west point of Île du Bic (bird sanctuary). Decide to pass it on south-west side as Lowrance shows stronger opposing currents on north side.

16h22: wind almost astern so we don't use the working jib. Bilge water is full of oil, suspect transmission.

Although the appearance of oil in the bilge is concerning there is little we can do at this part of the trip to effect repairs to Bagatelle's drive-train. At times like this, Don consults his "library" of books, leaflets and other printed material for information on nearest locations with a marine mechanic, supply stores, shore services, etc. Finding the right skill-set is not so problematic as we are are close to a number of fishing towns and villages. The long pole in the tent is the availability of repair parts specific to Bagatelle's systems. The best we would be able to do in this area is get the boat to a marina and put in an order for parts with whichever courier delivers at this location. Our experience on previous trips suggests we'll be in for long wait-times should any parts have to be put on-order. The Skipper decides to press onwards regardless of the condition of the engine or transmission.

18h05: Don goes to sleep after Eric wakes up. Don fell over while sitting in the cockpit from being so tired.

19h00: vessel off our stern, alter course 90° to starboard to let freighter pass us. "Atlantic Erie" from Halifax.

19h45: coming up on S8 through Batture aux Vaches.

19h51: abeam of S8, SoG 4.6 kt, cold, 13°C tonight!

20h30: secure at fuel dock at Tadoussac.

The head loses suction numerous times throughout the day, oh joy of joys. I'm thinking ahead to our comfortable berth at Tadoussac where we'll be sheltered from some of the wind and biting cold. Arriving late in the evening we make the cut-off for fuel at 20h30, thanks to a courtesy radio call while inbound. Our supper tonight is left-over salmon and rice, still tasty from yesterday! We're docked alongside "Ino," a custom-built Sampson 40 owned by a man named Donald. He and his wife invite us aboard for drinks and are very helpful in getting Bagatelle provisioned with fresh water. The practice of docking alongside other boats is common for this part of the St Lawrence due to the large number of whale-watching tourists who flock to Tadoussac in the summer.

Boats shrouded in fog at Tadoussac.

## 03 August 2010, Tadoussac to Cap-à-l'Aigle

09h10: awake to a nice sunny Tadoussac morning, temp still hovering around 13°C.

Crew head into town for groceries, there's a store close to the marina with decent prices. The fog comes and goes as we make our way through town.

12h00: slip Tadoussac.

12h27: SoG is 8.18 kt! Foggy!

13h05: pass K56, SoG 2.43 kt, CoG 205°M.

13h37: fog disappears.

15h11: actual closing speed is 2.03 kt, several times over the last hour we're sailing backwards with jib and main. ETA at Cap-à-l'Aigle: 05h00 to 08h00 tomorrow. According to the wind direction indicator we aren't able to point as much into the wind as usual, there appears to be a 10° error in its reading.

15h25: course is changing for the better, wind shifting.

15h37: closing speed is 1.17 kt, ETA 16h30 tomorrow, will take working jib down.

16h00: wind 18.6 kt apparent off port bow.

16h27: main down, SoG 3.25 kt.

17h27: SoG 4.68, CoG 231°M. ETA 22h12, 22.7 NM remaining.

19h50: Alain notices turbulence then the depth sounder reads 14.0 ft from the water-line, something passes us underneath. We're abeam of Port au Saumon when it happens.

22h15: secure at Cap-à-l'Aigle.

We sit back and enjoy a rum and coke after refuelling the aft fuel tank from one of Don's jerry cans. The tank takes 20L of fuel. This is a small marina and none of the attendants are present when we arrive. A notice at the entrance to the marina indicates people should leave money and their contact info in an envelope on the "honour system." Don does a quick back-of-the-hand calculation as to how much we owe and then we make our deposit. The Skipper plans on leaving at 04h00 next morning to take advantage of the tides.

Do I shower or sleep? Sleep it is!

## 04 August 2010, Cap-à-l'Aigle to Québec

04h30: too foggy, will try to depart later. Head loses suction yet again, Don tries to go ashore. Gate is locked, no luck in using heads on shore.

06h00: slipped, still foggy.

06h39: pass sailboat 0.125 NM to port.

07h27: alter course to avoid freighter coming up on our stern. Radio contact and horn blasts. We pass each other within half NM without any visual contact whatsoever. Eric goes to sleep.

08h19: pass Cap de la Corneille.

08h30: close to Cap-aux-Oies.

09h26: "Mark's City" freighter passes to port, up-bound. Again, no sight of her.

10h38: pass Baie Saint-Paul.

10h55: beside GRLA "Polsteam" from Valetta.

Bagtelle is making slow and steady progress up-river towards Quebec City. The constant throb of her engine in this calm morning puts everyone into a slight trance. Awakened from my rest I run through all the things that need attending to on a regular basis on the boat. Two out of three people need to be on watch at all times given the thick fog we find ourselves in. I move out of the cabin to check each of the sheets and lines, verifying everything movable is secured to the deck. All is well outside and so I head back below to check on our progress. Seated at the chart table I check the GPS, charts and radar for our stand-off distance to the nearest point of land. We are well into the morning and lunch will need to be served soon. Everything aboard the boat is an evolution that repeats itself, over and over again.

11h20: sun starting to poke through the fog!

11h47: 30-plus kt of wind all of a sudden!

13h20: abeam l'Anse aux Vaches, SoG 2.0 kt.

No luck on this portion of our trip with either sail, frustrating as our opportunity to motor is hampered with a stubborn wind on our nose. Traveling with the tide helps but once it recedes we're at a greater disadvantage. Minutes turn into hours with a view of the same small white house perched along the edge of hill-side on the north shore of the St Lawrence. We bob precariously in the choppy water as the wind batters Bagatelle's sails. All of the crew take turns at the helm as the autopilot is no match for the current, wind and waves in this stretch of water. The St Lawrence opens wider and wider as we head westward while exposed to the cruel wind offering no hint of abating any time soon.

13h40: we get overtaken by four cigar boats heading downstream on our port-side.

14h46: pass K92, SoG 1.5 kt.

15h00: two sailboats pass us heading downstream, both have their mains down due to a squall warning between Île-aux-Coudres and Tadoussac.

15h16: pass Pointe du Débarquement, SoG 1.22 kt.

15h30: close to K96 and freighter "Federal Pioneer."

16h15: SoG 1.5 kt, CoG 236°M, 31.4 NM to YCdQ, ETA 12h00 to 13h00 tomorrow.

Our ground speed picks up as we round the southern point off Mount Ste Anne. Wind also dropping as well. A giant motor yacht speeds past us on our port-side, Don is neither pleased nor impressed as it leaves a wake bigger than a freighter. We're soon on a southern course up river, tracking a powerful return from the RACON[5] situated in the middle of the St Lawrence to aid ships' passage through the narrow channel. It is an impressive structure, towering well out of the water and quite sturdy in its appearance. I find it somewhat curious as I don't recall it from our earlier trips.

I make my way forward to use the head after supper. Lifting the seat I find flecks of excrement and toilet paper everywhere. Don swears it isn't from him. Clean-up is frustrating and almost pointless as I'm sprayed with all manner of foulness when attempting to flush. I love that toilet. Many attempts are made throughout our trip at re-priming and purging; we suspect something is lodged in the intake as a mere trickle of water emerges in the bowl with each pump.

Making my way topside to take over for Alain at the helm, the wind is back up and we're engulfed in a massive deluge. Water rushes down my collar, I reach up to tighten, rain now pours down my sleeve. Alain and I have great difficulty seeing marks through the melee. A freighter makes her way past on our stern, I'm mindful to stay outside the channel to let her pass. The current is quite strong and we're being pulled towards a red mark as I attempt to slow Bagatelle's engine in an effort to avoid the freighter. The engine sputters and Don calls up "don't stall it, don't stall it!" Easing the throttle forward brings it back into operation. Speed boats are zooming by on both sides as we make our way towards Québec.

---

[5] A RACON, or RAdar beaCON, is a device that assists mariners with navigating in congested water-ways when vessels are required to follow specific routes or remain within narrow channels of a broader stretch of water. When electromagnetic waves emitted from a ship's radar come into contact with one of these beacons, a distinctive pattern is emitted in a direction towards the vessel. The radar operator should then see this pattern on their screen, directing them on an appropriate course. In addition, Morse code is embedded in the return to provide further information to each radar-equipped vessel. The definition in this foot-note is licensed under a Creative Commons Attribution 3.0 License, original work copyright Wikipedia®: RACON, http://en.m.wikipedia.org/wiki/Racon, January 2015.

Don's third or fourth attempt to "prime" the head. So. Much. Fun!

The city of Québec is adorned on a hillside with many thousands of lights shimmering through the darkness. Don is down below, looking at the GPS with a magnifying glass while Alain tries to help me de-conflict all of the lights on shore. Although we're out of the rain, our passage is difficult as we struggle to identify one flashing light from so many stop-lights, cars and other effects on shore. We pass several marks where Don wants me to call out their number; I bring the boat almost on top of them before we're able to identify. Current in this part of the river is strong! I come a little too close to one can on the south side of the Merchant Marine Academy and make the uncomfortable realization Bagatelle's engine isn't effective against the rising tide. All of the buoys are bowed over sideways in the rushing water. Given their size and weight there is little doubt as to the awesome power of the tides in this part of the St Lawrence!

A ferry comes up on our position after leaving the Lévis side of the river. Don is down below as we keep a watchful eye on it. The encroaching vessel alters starboard and is coming across our bow! I ask Alain for guidance and he recommends we come about. Lowering our speed we make a sharp turn to starboard and attempt to head back down river. I'm worried we won't have enough power to avoid the other vessel but with application of throttle we're making progress away from it despite the tide. Back enroute to YCdQ, I'm going by memory from reviewing charts prior to taking over at the helm.

Don takes over at the helm on our final approach to the yacht club. We get on their range and I'm forward with the spotlight trying to make the large formation of rocks on both sides of the entrance. Don is coming in fast in an effort to combat the effect of the tide; I think our approach is out-of-the-ordinary. We pass through the narrow inlet and I bellow "hard astern, hard astern!" Just in time for us to miss two powerboats off our bow.

We arrive at YCdQ at 23h59. Their floating docks are sheltered from wind and waves by an enormous breakwater: crew is aware of how warm it is compared to earlier portions of our trip. I remove my soaked rain-gear and make best efforts to keep all water as aft as possible. Rum and coke to cap off the evening. Before nodding off, Don calls out "almost makes you want to be back in Tadoussac." My response: "I can dump ice water on you if you want."

The following day is enjoyable albeit hot as we tour through Québec. Skipper and crew visit a marine hardware store close to YCdQ prior to heading into the city. A brand-new head sits on display as we enter the store. Although it is priced at $174.00, Don elects to wait until he's back in Kingston before committing to a replacement. Thoughts are screaming in my mind "buy it! For God's sake man, buy it!!"

I pick up a Tilley hat in the afternoon to ward off the sun. We head back to the yacht club after supper, picking up groceries along the way. Not wanting to splurge on taxis, everyone humps bags of food several blocks, around the Plains of Abraham and down a steep hill. The sky although darkened by night-fall is full of an ominous green glow with malevolent clouds roiling above the city highlighted by bursts of lightning. The air is as still as ever once I'm back aboard Bagatelle. Don and Alain will be back after their visit to the yacht club to hit the heads. I search the cabin and cockpit lockers for Don's heater to put it on "fan" mode in the hope of pushing hot and sticky air around us as we sleep. I'm out in the cockpit behind the helm when the wind picks up. Nothing too alarming at first, but within ten seconds all Hell breaks loose. Every boat in the yacht club is heeled over and the boat is pounded from stem to stern. Wind is roaring as if to herald the end of the world! I crawl under the wheel as a tremendous force is doing its damnedest to suck me out of the boat. A brief reprive signals my opportunity to head inside and so I dive for the cabin. Holding onto the rail next to the stove it's all I can do to remain standing as Bagatelle once again rocks and shakes in the fierce and strong wind!

The turmoil is over as soon as it starts. Making my way topside, several items are missing including my brand-new hat. Sonofabitch! A fellow boater declares the boat's stern is away from the dock, her stern line has parted. I head onto the dock, secure the stern with two lines then resume looking for Don's blue flashlight to look for missing items.

Scanning the opposing embankment with nothing in sight I'm left thinking the hat has made its way over and is now floating on the St Lawrence with the tide. Scanning the water, back towards the fuel dock there's something floating close to the dock that looks like a hat. Heading towards the entry to the fuel dock I meet Don and Alain at the main gate. Don held onto the gate railing when the wind struck. He tells us the railing felt ready to fly away; the door closed with an awful "bang!" after he scrambled onto dry land.

Mindful of the wind picking up again at any second I make my way down the steep embankment, cutting my hand on rocks as I go. Other than being soaked in seawater the hat is none the worse for wear. Turns out there's a piece of foam inside the small pouch of the hat to aid with floatation. Tilley Endurables sure makes decent kit!

## Afterward

Like all trips aboard the boat, this one has its share of challenges. From our departure at Gaspé the wind is on our nose every hour we're at sea. With the exception of a few glorious minutes of true sailing the engine and transmission are in full commission for hours on end. The trend doesn't continue: Bagatelle's engine and transmission quit on Don when they are outside of Longueil. The boat is out of water for a while; repairs don't hold. Don ends up getting towed for a portion of his return trip to Kingston with further delays in Brockville, ON.

| Depart | Arrive | Accum Time on Boat [days] | Accum Time Underway [hours] | Accum Engine Time [hours] | Accum Distance [NM] | Average Speed [kt] |
|---|---|---|---|---|---|---|
| Gaspé | Rivière-au-Renard | 1 | 14.3 | 3.6 | 41.6 | 2.9 |
| Rivière-au-Renard | Sainte-Anne-des-Monts | 2 | 31.5 | 20.9 | 137.7 | 5.6 |
| Sainte-Anne-des-Monts | Rimouski | 3 | 48.0 | 37.3 | 231.6 | 5.7 |
| Rimouski | Tadoussac | 4 | 57.9 | 47.5 | 287.3 | 5.6 |
| Tadoussac | Cap-à-l'Aigle | 5 | 68.1 | 57.6 | 324.5 | 3.6 |
| Cap-à-l'Aigle | Québec | 6 | 86.1 | 76.0 | 400.1 | 4.2 |

Engine Time vs Time Underway: 88.3%
Time Underway vs Time on Boat: 63.2%

Table 6. Trip summary for Bagatelle's voyage from Gaspé, QC to Québec, QC in 2010.

# Chapter 7

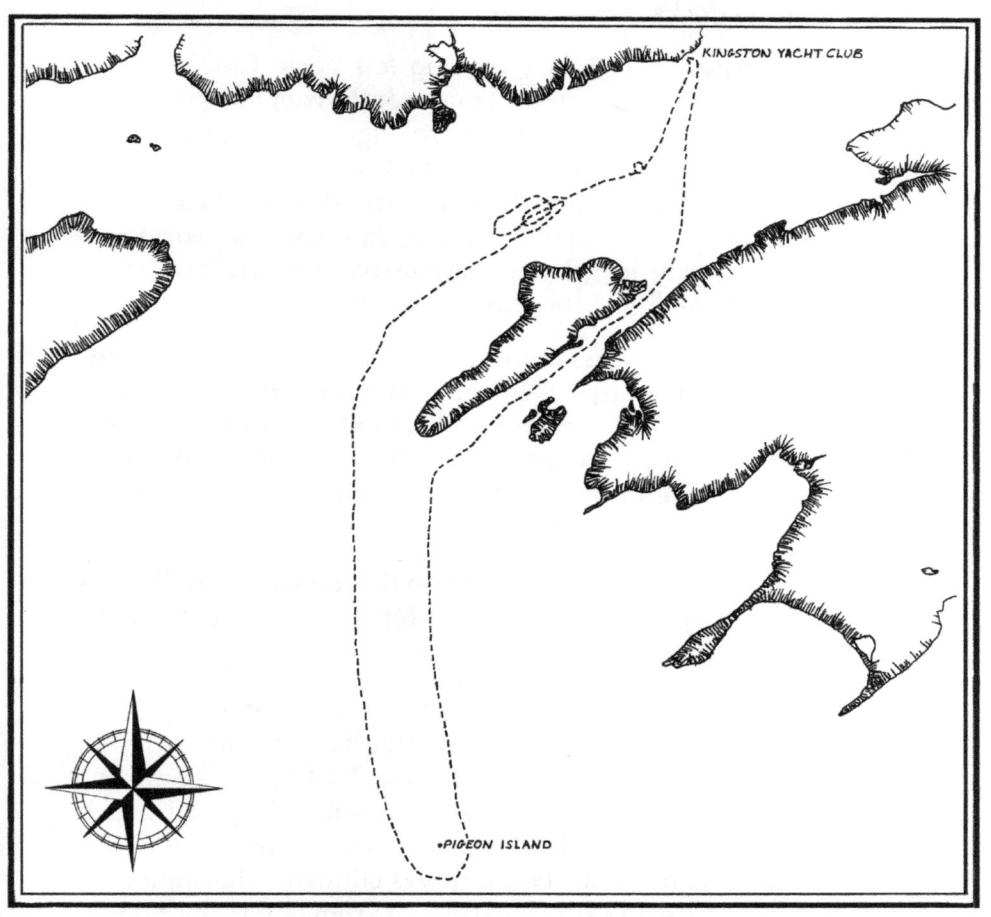

*Pigeon Island Race, Kingston, ON*

25 May 2013

The sky is a bright blue as I make my way towards Kingston for our 09h30 start. Don, Chris and a few others are at KYC when I arrive. Don's red van is parked close to Bagatelle. This might be the last season he can park this close since KYC wants to put out more floating docks.

The Pigeon Island race is one of Kingston Yacht Club's annual events. It is held in May, around one month from the start of the sailing season. I participated in several Pigeon Island races prior to 2013. The race in each of those years saw little wind and we therefore elected to come about and return to the yacht club in the late afternoon. The course for Pigeon Island has slight variations year-to-year and its length is 19 NM on average. There is a time limit of 24h00 the day of the race.

As we make preparations to leave the yacht club, I discover the mast for the wind charger is laying in the cockpit. With twenty minutes before the start of the race I scramble back to my car to find appropriate tools to secure it. We're out of our mooring, motoring for the entrance to the club when I get everything reconnected.

Wind is coming up strong as we put up the main and jib. There's confusion amongst crew as we make for the start line; then, the horn sounds and the race is underway!

Chris suggests flying a spinnaker on our first leg; Don recommends the 1 1/2 weight. I head to the bow and haul up what I believe to be the correct one. I confirm with Chris before moving up to the pulpit to make ready to raise sails. The sail bag is secured, the spinnaker halyard is secured to its head, the port guy is clipped and then the starboard guy is clipped. The spinnaker pole goes into place on Don's mast. I try to remember what has to happen next to hoist this gigantic balloon of a sail. We're soon ready and commence hoisting when Chris calls "stop!"

With strong gusts of wind, the halyard has become twisted around the top shroud with the spinnaker almost reaching the top. Damn. Not having any success in freeing it we call for the errant hoist to be brought down enough to come free. It gets lowered too much and now the spin is in the water. Chris and I wrestle to get the clew and bottom of this massive sail on deck. As the halyard is righted we notice a small tear developing close to the tack of the sail.

A huge gust of wind bears down on us and we dip the boom for the main in the water! Righted, someone calls out to lower the spinnaker. The jib is still up at this point so I don't notice the giant gaping hole until most of the spinnaker is back on deck. A big section of it has blown out and is now floating aft of Bagatelle. We come about and head back towards KYC for its recovery. In our haste to recover the torn section we approach too close and Bagatelle goes right over top of it. We come about one more time and pick it up on second attempt. The wind is gusting strong!

Back on course, we stay on a southward tack, all the way to Pigeon Island. We have enough time for soup and sandwiches before we come around the island.

Don lets me take the helm after we pass Pigeon Island. The wind is icy cold but I feel jubilation as we rock through the waves. A copious amount of water comes crashing over the bow and our port rail is dipping well below the water-line from time-to-time. With 30-plus kt of wind, we're making a good 7 kt! Bagatelle is having a hard time keeping pointed but nothing too extreme to keep us away from our intended course. This is great sailing!

We come about and head for the entrance to the channel between Simcoe Island and Wolfe Island. Don takes the helm when I mention we're getting close to land and the channel is narrowing. Keeping Bagatelle pointed on an optimum course is all fine and good; however, we're getting closer and closer to a bunch of rocks and my comfort zone is diminishing just as quick.

We pass the cable ferry without any drama and are soon tacking through two buoys on our final leg. The wind picks up again after leaving shelter of the island. The previous two Pigeon Island races are in sharp contrast to this cold air and incredible wind. After completing one of the legs Chris notices the starboard track for the jib sheet is lifting off the deck. We re-secure things using Don's second rail.

Back at KYC, the winch for the main halyard is coming apart and crew notice significant tears in both the main and jib. This is a punishing trip!

## Afterward

This is one of Bagatelle's shortest and most expensive excursions in terms of the extent of damage to her sails and structure. Races such as these demand all crew have lots of experience with each evolution. Flying a spinnaker can be difficult at the best of times when crew are not trained and experienced. My infrequent trips aboard the boat didn't help our situation on this race. That being said we all enjoyed ouselves once Bagatelle's sails and rigging were under control and trimmed to accommodate the condition of the winds. As I am moving east this summer, this is my last excursion aboard Bagatelle for some time to come.

# Epilogue

I trust you enjoyed the chapters in this book and you experienced the many ups and downs of an amazing set of voyages on the Great Lakes, St Lawrence Seaway and Canadian East Coast. The below table is a summary of each trip in Chapters 1 through 6. Chapter 7 is not included as it is a one-day race by Kingston and Wolfe Island.

| Depart | Arrive | Accum Time on Boat [days] | Accum Time Underway [hours] | Accum Engine Time [hours] | Accum Distance [NM] | Average Speed [kt] |
|---|---|---|---|---|---|---|
| Halifax | Kingston | 26 | 327.6 | 187.6 | 1,405.7 | 4.7 |
| Québec | Baddeck | 11 | 157.4 | 69.7 | 845.8 | 4.6 |
| Charlottetown | Sainte-Anne-des-Monts | 6 | 88.9 | 42.1 | 453.0 | 4.3 |
| Québec | Rimouski | 2 | 33.6 | 22.4 | 168.5 | 4.3 |
| Kingston | McGregor Bay | 10 | 158.3 | 108.8 | 697.1 | 5.9 |
| Gaspé | Québec | 6 | 86.1 | 76.0 | 400.1 | 4.2 |
| | Grand Totals | 61 | 852.0 | 506.6 | 3970.2 | 4.7 |

Table 7. Summary of trips for Chapters 1 through 6.

Two notional trips are presented in the appendices of this book using the average speed in Table 7. The first appendix contains information on a round-trip from Kingston, ON to Cornerbrook Newfoundland, over to Cape Breton Island, further west to Halifax, NS then back to Kingston, ON. The second appendix is a trip from Kingston, ON to McGregor Bay, ON and back.

Both appendices show the total cost per trip. They also show the cost of each trip over a fifteen-year period, assuming one trip every two years in each appendix. All together, over this same period the number of crew that have sailed aboard Bagatelle is 136. Not taking into account inflation, the total cost is greater than 1.5 million Canadian dollars (CDN).

Two truths emerge from the estimates in the appendices. (1) To quote Mark from my very first long-distance trip aboard Bagatelle: "a boat is a pit you throw money into." (2) Don has his own Navy!

There are quite a few entries from Bagatelle's log that didn't make it into this book, and readers are reminded that it covers only a fraction of each of the major trips Don and Bagatelle have undertaken since 2001. You can see from the estimates in the appendices, a whole host of other crew must have their own stories and experiences. As this book draws to a close I put the challenge out to each and every one of the other crew to print your own encounters and adventures aboard Bagatelle!

For those who haven't done any long-distance sailing (assuming you've made it this far in the book), about the only thing left to do is go and make your own adventures aboard a sail-boat if you have not already had the opportunity to do so. I'll go ahead and state the obvious: make sure you team up with one or more folks who have a lot of experience with the type of sailing you intend to partake in! It also helps if your boat is ship-shape with a bullet-proof engine and drivetrain! For those who've set sail on long-endurance courses may you encounter only the most favourable winds and may the seas forever roll beneath your feet.

# Appendix 1: Maritimes Trip

| Depart | Arrive | Accum Distance [NM] | Accum Stops |
|---|---|---|---|
| Kingston | Butternut Bay | 37.63 | 1 |
| Butternut Bay | Nairne Island | 80.83 | 2 |
| Nairne Island | Cornwall | 95.03 | 3 |
| Cornwall | Royal St Lawrence Yacht Club | 145.79 | 4 |
| Royal St Lawrence Yacht Club | Batiscan | 247.84 | 5 |
| Batiscan | Québec | 294.82 | 6 |
| Québec | Cap-à-l'Aigle | 370.41 | 7 |
| Cap-à-l'Aigle | Tadoussac | 407.67 | 8 |
| Tadoussac | Rimouski | 463.28 | 9 |
| Rimouski | Rivière-au-Renard | 652.81 | 10 |
| Rivière-au-Renard | Cornerbrook | 914.69 | 11 |
| Cornerbrook | Codroy | 1039.96 | 12 |
| Codroy | North Sydney | 1149.57 | 13 |
| North Sydney | Baddeck | 1190.66 | 14 |
| Baddeck | St Peter's | 1220.68 | 15 |
| St Peter's | Port Hawkesbury | 1246.87 | 16 |
| Port Hawkesbury | Canso | 1272.79 | 17 |
| Canso | Whitehead Harbour | 1295.46 | 18 |
| Whitehead Harbour | Liscombe Harbour | 1347.84 | 19 |
| Liscombe Harbour | Sheet Harbour | 1,387.3 | 20 |
| Sheet Harbour | Halifax | 1,451.5 | 21 |
| Halifax | Lunenburg | 1,508.7 | 22 |
| Lunenburg | Halifax | 1,566.0 | 23 |
| Halifax | Sheet Harbour | 1,630.2 | 24 |
| Sheet Harbour | Liscombe Harbour | 1,669.7 | 25 |
| Liscombe Harbour | Whitehead Harbour | 1,722.0 | 26 |
| Whitehead Harbour | Canso | 1,744.7 | 27 |
| Canso | Port Hawkesbury | 1,770.6 | 28 |
| Port Hawkesbury | D'Escousse | 1,793.0 | 29 |
| D'Escousse | St Peter's | 1,799.0 | 30 |
| St Peter's | Corbett's Cove | 1,800.9 | 31 |
| Corbett's Cove | Dundee | 1,820.1 | 32 |
| Dundee | St Peter's | 1,841.3 | 33 |
| St Peter's | Port Hawkesbury | 1,867.8 | 34 |
| Port Hawkesbury | Charlottetown | 1,961.7 | 35 |
| Charlottetown | Îles-de-la-Madeleine | 2,105.3 | 36 |
| Îles-de-la-Madeleine | Gaspé | 2,277.1 | 37 |
| Gaspé | Matane | 2,459.6 | 38 |
| Matane | Rimouski | 2,508.4 | 39 |
| Rimouski | Tadoussac | 2,564.0 | 40 |
| Tadoussac | Cap-à-l'Aigle | 2,601.3 | 41 |
| Cap-à-l'Aigle | Québec | 2,676.9 | 42 |
| Québec | Batiscan | 2,723.9 | 43 |
| Batiscan | Royal St Lawrence Yacht Club | 2,825.9 | 44 |
| Royal St Lawrence Yacht Club | Cornwall | 2,876.7 | 45 |
| Cornwall | Nairne Island | 2,890.9 | 46 |
| Nairne Island | Butternut Bay | 2,934.1 | 47 |
| Butternut Bay | Kingston | 2,971.7 | 48 |

Trip Distance (td), [NM]  2,971.7

Table 8a. Summary for a round-trip to the Maritimes from Kingston, ON aboard Bagatelle.

## 142  Knots Made Good

| Variables (See Note 1) | Min | Max | Remarks |
|---|---|---|---|
| Speed-over-Ground (sog), [kt] | 4.1 | 5.1 | Distances and speeds expressed in nautical miles and knots respectively. |
| Time Underway (tu), [hours/trip] | 582.7 | 724.8 | tu = td/sog |
| Slack Factor (sf), [time_on_boat/time_underway] | 2.0 | 2.1 | Amount of time spent on the boat versus amount of time spent underway. |
| Time on Boat (tob), [days/trip] | 48.6 | 63.4 | tob = tu*sf/24 |
| Crew (c), [people] | 3 | 5 | Number of crew required for each rotation (roto). |
| Crew Turn-over (ct), [%] | 50% | 75% | Crew turn-over each roto versus total number of crew on-board. |
| Roto Length (rl), [days] | 5 | 10 | Amount of time between crew changes. |
| No-show Margin (nsm), [%] | 10% | 15% | Ratio of no-show crew to required crew. |
| Total Required Crew (trc), [people/trip] | 20 | 34 | trc = c*(1 + tob*ct/rl)*(1 + nsm), rounded up. |
| Number of Trips per Year (nt), [trip/year] | 0.5 | 0.5 | One trip every two years. |
| Number of Years Sailing (ny), [year] | 15 | 15 | Number of years sailing this trip. |
| Crew Turn-over Year-over-Year (ctyoy), [%] | 10% | 15% | Percentage of crew turn-over from one year to the next. |
| Total Required Crew for this Epoch (trce), [people] | 35 | 73 | trce = trc*(1 + nt*ny*ctyoy), rounded up. |
| Engine Run Factor (erf), [%] | 65% | 75% | Amount of time engine is run versus time underway. |
| Engine Time (et), [hours] | 378.7 | 543.6 | et = tu*erf |
| Fuel Burn Rate (fbr), [L/hr] | 2.0 | 2.5 | Bagatelle burns approximately 2.0 L/hr at 2100 RPM. |
| Fuel Required (fr), [L] | 757.5 | 1,359.0 | fr = et*fbr |
| Fuel Price (fp), [CAD/L] | 1.50 | 2.00 | Prices vary considerably from stop-to-stop. |
| Fuel Cost (fc), [CAD] | 1,136.24 | 2,718.02 | fc = fr*fp |
| Cost to Transit through Locks/Canals [CAD] | 300.00 | 300.00 | $30.00/lock, 16 locks each trip. |
| Docking Fees [CAD] | 3,517.80 | 3,517.80 | $2.75/foot multiplied by 41-foot LWL, total # stops, 65% dock availability at each stop. |
| Food [CAD] | 7,488.00 | 12,480.00 | $80.00/person multiplied by # crew each trip portion, total # stops, 65% store availability. |
| Cost to Transport Crew to Each Stop [CAD] | 30,000.00 | 51,000.00 | $1500.00/person average cost multiplied by # crew per trip. |
| Trip Cost (p), [CAD] | 42,442.04 | 70,015.82 | See Note 2. |
| Trip Cost for this Epoch (pe), [CAD] | 636,630.61 | 1,050,237.36 | pe = p*ny |

Notes:
1. Nomenclature for variables is: variable name (abbreviated name), [units]
2. Trip cost (p) does not take into account insurance, maintenance, boat up-keep, fees at home yacht club, long-term storage, etc.

Table 8b. Summary of costs and crewing numbers for a round-trip to the Maritimes from Kingston, ON aboard Bagatelle.

# Appendix 2: McGregor Bay Trip

| Depart | Arrive | Accum Distance [NM] | Accum Stops |
|---|---|---|---|
| Kingston | Port Weller | 143.1 | 1 |
| Port Weller | Port Colborne | 165.3 | 2 |
| Port Colborne | Port Dover | 211.9 | 3 |
| Port Dover | Leamington | 364.7 | 4 |
| Leamington | Windsor | 406.6 | 5 |
| Windsor | Sarnia | 467.1 | 6 |
| Sarnia | Kincardine | 551.8 | 7 |
| Kincardine | Tobermory | 633.4 | 8 |
| Tobermory | McGregor Bay | 697.1 | 9 |
| McGregor Bay | Tobermory | 760.8 | 10 |
| Tobermory | Kincardine | 842.3 | 11 |
| Kincardine | Sarnia | 927.1 | 12 |
| Sarnia | Windsor | 987.6 | 13 |
| Windsor | Leamington | 1,029.4 | 14 |
| Leamington | Port Dover | 1,182.2 | 15 |
| Port Dover | Port Colborne | 1,228.8 | 16 |
| Port Colborne | Port Weller | 1,251.1 | 17 |
| Port Weller | Kingston | 1,394.2 | 18 |

Trip Distance (td), [NM]  1,394.2

Table 9a. Summary for a round-trip to McGregor Bay, ON from Kingston, ON aboard Bagatelle.

| Variables (See Note 1) | Min | Max | Remarks |
|---|---|---|---|
| Speed-over-Ground (sog), [kt] | 4.1 | 5.1 | Distances and speeds expressed in nautical miles and knots respectively. |
| Time Underway (tu), [hours/trip] | 273.4 | 340.0 | tu = td/sog |
| Slack Factor (sf), [time_on_boat/time_underway] | 2.0 | 2.1 | Amount of time spent on the boat versus amount of time spent underway. |
| Time on Boat (tob), [days/trip] | 22.8 | 29.8 | tob = tu*sf/24 |
| Crew (c), [people] | 3 | 5 | Number of crew required for each rotation (roto). |
| Crew Turn-over (ct), [%] | 50% | 75% | Crew turn-over each roto versus total number of crew on-board. |
| Roto Length (rl), [days] | 5 | 10 | Amount of time between crew changes. |
| No-show Margin (nsm), [%] | 10% | 15% | Ratio of no-show crew to required crew. |
| Total Required Crew (trc), [people/trip] | 11 | 19 | trc = c*(1 + tob*ct/rl)*(1 + nsm), rounded up. |
| Number of Trips per Year (nt), [trip/year] | 0.5 | 0.5 | One trip every two years. |
| Number of Years Sailing (ny), [year] | 15 | 15 | Number of years sailing this trip. |
| Crew Turn-over Year-over-Year (ctyoy), [%] | 10% | 15% | Percentage of crew turn-over from one year to the next. |
| Total Required Crew for this Epoch (trce), [people] | 20 | 41 | trce = trc*(1 + nt*ny*ctyoy), rounded up. |
| Engine Run Factor (erf), [%] | 65% | 75% | Amount of time engine is run versus time underway. |
| Engine Time (et), [hours] | 177.7 | 255.0 | et = tu*erf |
| Fuel Burn Rate (fbr), [L/hr] | 2.0 | 2.5 | Bagatelle burns approximately 2.0 L/hr at 2100 RPM. |
| Fuel Required (fr), [L] | 355.4 | 637.6 | fr = et*fbr |
| Fuel Price (fp), [CAD/L] | 1.50 | 2.00 | Prices vary considerably from stop-to-stop. |
| Fuel Cost (fc), [CAD] | 533.06 | 1,275.15 | fc = fr*fp |
| Cost to Transit through Locks/Canals [CAD] | 480.00 | 480.00 | $30.00/lock, 16 locks each trip. |
| Docking Fees [CAD] | 1,319.18 | 1,319.18 | $2.75/foot multiplied by 41-foot LWL, total # stops, 65% dock availability at each stop. |
| Food [CAD] | 2,808.00 | 4,680.00 | $80.00/person multiplied by # crew each trip portion, total # stops, 65% store availability. |
| Cost to Transport Crew to Each Stop [CAD] | 16,500.00 | 28,500.00 | $1500.00/person average cost multiplied by # crew per trip. |
| Trip Cost (p), [CAD] | 22,600.24 | 37,214.33 | See Note 2. |
| Trip Cost for this Epoch (pe), [CAD] | 339,003.59 | 558,214.94 | pe = p*ny |

Notes:
1. Nomenclature for variables is: variable name (abbreviated name), [units]
2. Trip cost (p) does not take into account insurance, maintenance, boat up-keep, fees at home yacht club, long-term storage, etc.

Table 9b. Summary of costs and crewing numbers for a round-trip to McGregor Bay, ON from Kingston, ON aboard Bagatelle.

148   Knots Made Good

# Appendix 3: Bagatelle – A Living History

## BAGATELLE

**BAGATELLE HAS HAD A LONG AND DISTINGUISHED RACING AND CRUISING CAREER SAILING OUT OF THE KINGSTON YACHT CLUB**

After the obvious success of *Red Jacket*, Cuthbertson & Cassian again teamed up with Erich Bruckmann to produce the Redline 41 in series production, that is, built out of a mould. *Bagatelle*, built in 1969 for Mr. Allan Taylor, was the first of the Mk II configurations, featuring a filled out back end, often referred to as a "bustle". In 1969 the Royal Canadian Yacht Club accepted a challenge from Cleveland Yachting Club for the Canada's Cup, with RCYC producing three potential defenders, all designed by Cuthbertson & Cassian – *Bagatelle*, *True North*, and *Manitou*. *Manitou* won the defender trials, and went on to defeat the US challenger *Niagara* 4-0. *Bagatelle* has had a long and distinguished racing and cruising career sailing out of the Kingston Yacht Club under the ownership of Mr. Don Curry. Over 20 Redline 41s were built, with Redline 41 *Condor* repeating *Red Jacket's* overall victory at SORC in 1972.

### Specifications:

Designer:
Cuthbertson & Cassian
Builder:
Bruckmann Manufacturing
LOA: 41.42 ft
LWL: 30 ft

Beam: 11.17 ft
Displ.: 19,700
Sail area: 726 sq ft
Draught: 6.75 ft
Ballast: 9500 lbs

# References

Dog Watch, http://en.wikipedia.org/wiki/Dog_watch, February 2015

LORAN, http://en.wikipedia.org/wiki/LORAN, January 2015

"Ontario-based sloop under escort in rough seas between Quebec and PEI," The Canadian Press, 8 August 2007 11:19 AM ET

RACON, http://en.m.wikipedia.org/wiki/Racon, January 2015

# Glossary

*accum*, accumulated

*autohelm (autopilot)*, self-steering equipment on-board a boat or ship

*CDN*, Canadian dollars

*CoG*, course-over-ground

*clew*, the after lower corner of a sail

*°C*, degrees Celsius

*°F*, degrees Fahrenheit

*°M*, degrees magnetic

*dry*, empty (as in a ship without cargo)

*ETA*, expected time-of-arrival

*forestay (headstay)*, a cable that runs from the bow to the upper part of the mast; as in: our headsail attaches to the headstay.

*ft*, foot

*genoa ("genny")*, large foresail (headsail) whose clew extends beyond the foretriangle (mast).

*GPS*, global positioning system

*halyard*, line that raises a sail

*head*, (1) top corner of a triangular sail; (2) bathroom (toilet) on a boat; (3) front of the boat

*jib*, foresail that fits inside the fore-triangle (not extending beyond the mast)

*jibe*, to turn the stern of the boat through the eye of the wind

*kt*, nautical mile per hour ("knot")

*KYC*, Kingston Yacht Club

*L*, Litre

*line*, braided rope/cord with a thickness derived from the context of its use

*LORAN*, LOng RAnge Navigation

*LWL*, length at water-line

*MAFOR*, MArine FORecast

*NS*, Nova Scotia

*NM*, nautical mile (1 nautical mile = 1.852 kilometers = 1.151 US statute miles

*ON*, Ontario

*PEI*, Prince Edward Island

*QC*, Québec

*RACON*, RAdar beaCON

*range*, (1) the difference between high and low tide; (2) the extent of a light's visibility; (3) when two objects line up, also called a transit, that may indicate a channel; as in: "We will know to turn into the channel when the range lights line up"

*RPM*, revolutions-per-minute

*RMCC*, Royal Military College of Canada

*SoG*, speed-over-ground

*port*, (1) left side when looking forward; (2) window in the side of the boat; (3) where boats come in to dock

*sail-tie*, line two to three arms in length used for securing a furled sail to the boom or deck of a boat

*sheet*, a line that controls a sail with one end tied to the clew of the sail

*starboard*, the right side facing forward

*spinnaker*, A large (often colourful) balloon-shaped sail flown from the head of a boat

*tack*, (1) to change direction by putting the bow through the eye of the wind; (2) side of the boat opposite the side the boom is on; (3) forward lower corner of a sail

*tacking*, act of changing from port to starboard tack and vice-versa

*UPS*, United Parcel Service

*USA*, United States of America

*USNA*, United States Naval Academy

*YCdQ*, Yacht Club de Québec

www.ingramcontent.com/pod-product-compliance
Lightning Source LLC
Chambersburg PA
CBHW032047090426
42744CB00004B/113